What the experts are saying about this book!

Dr. Tuckman continues to do an exceptional job of distilling the essence of theory and science about ADHD into a very practical guide for the adult with ADHD.

> *Russell Barkley, PhD*
> *Clinical Professor of Psychiatry*
> *Medical University of South Carolina (Charleston)*

Dr. Tuckman's book *Understand Your Brain, Get More Done* provides realistic, practical, and useful information for those with adult ADHD. Not only is the book enlightening, but it is also fun to read. The exercises in the book are educational, easy to complete, and give great insight into the world of adult ADHD. I have recommended Dr. Tuckman's companion book *More Attention, Less Deficit* to my patients and clients, and I have listed it as a recommended resource in my books due to its straightforward nature and wealth of information. I will recommend *Understand Your Brain, Get More Done* for the same reasons. They are both outstanding books.

> *Stephanie Moulton Sarkis PhD, NCC, LMHC*
> *Psychotherapist*
> *Author of* 10 Simple Solutions to Adult ADD,
> Making the Grade with ADD,
> ADD and Your Money, *and*
> Adult ADD: A Guide for the Newly Diagnosed

Dr. Ari Tuckman's new book *Understand You Brain, Get More Done* is a great resource that clearly explains and illustrates how ADHD and executive function impacts the lives of adults with ADHD. He clearly explains what executive function is in concise and easy- to-understand language and presents excellent real- life examples to support each area of challenge.

What separates Dr. Tuckman's new book from so many of the other ADHD books on the market, are the practical exercises he presents for each of the main areas of executive function. He doesn't tell you what to do. He understands that your ADHD brain wiring is unique and you need to understand how it works so you can make it work for you. That's why Dr. Tuckman has created a WORK book; not just a book to be read and put on the shelf. He knows that for change to occur you have to work at it. If you do the work in *Understand Your Brain, Get More Done*, you will discover that your work will successfully work for you. It will significantly improve the quality of your life.

> *David Giwerc, MCC*
> *Founder & President, ADD Coach Academy*
> *Author of* Permission to Proceed: The Keys to Creating a Life of Passion, Purpose and Possibility for Adults with ADHD

Understand Your Brain, Get More Done is a straightforward, jargon-free, refreshing workbook—a must for any adult with ADHD. Dr. Tuckman presents valuable scientific information in the most approachable way possible. Adults with ADHD will not be bored, but instead be challenged and enlightened by this structured, information-packed workbook. The book's tone is non-judgmental, empathic and even humorous at times. Most importantly, Dr. Tuckman gets it. He does not waste the ADHD reader's time with exercises that sound good on paper but in the real world are useless. This is the workbook I will use with my ADHD clients.

> *Roberto Olivardia, Ph.D.*
> *Clinical Instructor of Psychology, Department of Psychiatry, Harvard Medical School*
> *Clinical Associate in Psychology, McLean Hospital*
> *Private Practice, Belmont, Massachusetts*

Ari Tuckman has written a truly useful, insightful guide to working with, through, and even around (when necessary) your ADHD brain.

> *Thom Hartmann*
> New York Times *bestselling author of 23 books, including* The Edison Gene *and*
> ADD: A Different Perception

This workbook provides a step-by-step guide to a new, more consistent future you may never have thought possible. Is there work involved? Of course! They don't call it a work-book for nothing. But Tuckman is right on target with his explanations and strategies—I can't wait to recommend it to my couples clients!

> *Melissa Orlov*
> *Author of the award-winning* The ADHD Effect on Marriage: Understand and Rebuild Your Relationship in Six Steps

Understand Your Brain, Get More Done

The ADHD Executive Functions Workbook

Ari Tuckman, PsyD, MBA

Specialty Press, Inc.
300 N.W. 70th Ave., Suite 102
Plantation, Florida 33317

Cover Design: Michael Wall, Kall Graphics
Layout: Babs Kall, Kall Graphics

Specialty Press, Inc.
300 Northwest 70th Avenue, Suite 102
Plantation, Florida 33317
(954) 792-8100 • (800) 233-9273

Printed in the United States of America

ISBN-13: 978-1886941-39-7

ISBN-10: 1-886941-39-4

Table of Contents

Acknowledgments

As always, there are many people to acknowledge. First, I want to thank my publisher, Harvey Parker, for coming up with the idea to do an executive functions workbook and giving me another reason to work with him. He's a man of many ideas. I would also like to thank Babs Kall and Mike Wall for once again doing all the graphic design work and making plain old words look good.

I want to thank my friends and colleagues for their feedback and suggestions and being willing to look at early versions (which I'm now kind of embarrassed about): Deb Rowley, Roberto Olivardia, Stephanie Sarkis, Comfort Belbas (and her adult ADHD support group), Laurie Pogach, Linda Roggli, and Mark Bertin. The world of ADHD is a small one. It's good to have friends.

Finally, and again, I want to thank my wife Heather. I keep writing books, and she keeps being a good sport about it. Hopefully neither one of us runs out of steam any time soon.

Other Books by Ari Tuckman

Integrative Treatment for Adult ADHD:
A Practical, Easy-to-Use Guide for Clinicians (2007)
New Harbinger Publications

More Attention, Less Deficit:
Success Strategiges for Adults with ADHD (2009)
Specialty Press, Inc.

Dedication

For Heather—my wife,
my friend,
my partner,
my love.

Foreword

Quick! Read this before you decide to put this book back on the shelf!

Or read this before you put it down "to get back to later", or toss it onto your bonfire pile of unread books, or stick it under a table leg to balance your wobbly picnic table.

See, I understand. I hate workbooks, too. Just the term, workbook. Think about it. Who wants to work a book, or who wants a book about work? Plus, it brings back memories. Oh, does it ever bring back memories. I was lucky. I actually loved school, because I had such great teachers. *But I hated workbooks.* They were invariably…boring. And I hate boring. Workbooks all but defined boring. They always had the drabbest, most unimaginative covers, they were flimsily bound, always on the verge of falling apart, and the paper stock was always so absorbent that ambient moisture quickly waterlogged the workbook, unless you kept it in a drawer of salt, which I did not ever do. Oh, such memories. I can see them now, those workbooks.

And I can hear some teacher saying, "Now open your workbooks to page…" That was my cue to let my mind wander. I would sit staring into the workbook, while my mind conjured up many other wonderful worlds. I suppose in that sense I did like workbooks. They offered me a prod to leave this world for a glorious other one. So I should take it back. Workbooks, you're okay in my book.

To add to my new improved opinion of workbooks, I saw *this* workbook by Dr. Ari Tuckman. To start, look at what the title promises the book will do: *Understand Your Brain, Get More Done.* In today's information age, it's all about brain power, so the better you know your brain, the better you'll do. This is where the executive functions come in (you might have heard of them). They're some of the best of what our brains do. As the cover says, they help us focus attention, control emotions, set priorities, manage time, plan activities, stay organized, and improve memory. That's quite a list! And that's not even everything they do!

If Dr. Ari Tuckman can produce a workbook that can help with all that stuff, then he's my man and it's my book. Guess what? *It does!* You have to give this workbook a chance. I know, you hate workbooks, we all hate workbooks, but you're going to love this one because it really is going to help you do stuff you really need to do and really do not want to have trouble with one day longer than you have to.

Why have difficulty with, say, managing time? Do you know that some people get fired and some people get divorced because they can't do that well? Can you imagine? Fired or divorced because they couldn't manage time? Now, I am sure this does not apply to you, I am sure you are a virtual grand master of the management of time, I am sure you would no more be late than fly to the moon, but just in case you might happen to know someone who actually does have the terribly embarrassing problem of *not* being able to manage time, then this workbook is for him! Or her! Or them!

Organization, planning, prioritizing, remembering…I know, these are all second nature for you and me, we wouldn't be caught dead forgetting something or losing something or misplacing a priority, but for those poor souls who actually do have trouble with these simple, elementary, so-easy-my-dog-can-do-it tasks, this workbook is for them! Slip it into their desk or under their door. However you do it, get it to them. And make sure they don't throw it on a pile before they read it!

This book could really change their lives for the better. Truly it could. I mean it. And I know what I'm talking about. Pretty cool, huh?

Edward Hallowell, MD
Director of the Hallowell Centers in Sudbury, MA and New York City

How to Use This Book—And How It's Different

There are three very important reasons that make this book different from other books—and why you should expect better results from it.

1. This is More Work than Book (Emphasis on Doing, Not Reading)

I have included a lot of exercises to help you get the most out of this workbook. You don't have to do any of the exercises, but the more you do, the more benefit you will get. The more you put in, the more you get out. You may find that some of the exercises resonate with you more than others do—this is totally normal. However, you may also find that some of the exercises are a fair bit of work. This is good. Change takes effort—you've already figured out all sorts of things, so you're left with only stuff that's going to take some work. You've come to the right place—this is a *work*book, and you're going to do some work! You may find it helpful to dedicate some regular time to this workbook, just as you would with a therapist or coach or going to the gym.

There are lots of books out there about ADHD (I've written two of them). And most of them have lots of good information. I felt the need to write a workbook this time because I wanted to help readers more directly make changes in their daily lives. This means actively trying the exercises, rather than simply reading a bunch of stuff that sounds good and makes sense but doesn't directly translate into your life. The exercises in this workbook bridge that gap between knowledge and action by giving you specific activities to practice.

Hopefully the work you put in on the exercises will be worth the improvements in your day to day life. That's the goal. I've worked really hard to give you meaningful exercises that aren't pointlessly easy, but also not so difficult that you need a masters degree in accounting to figure them out. So once again I'm trying to write the book that Goldilocks would choose—not too obvious but also not too confusing. This has been *much* harder than I had originally thought. It turns out that it's really hard to write a worthwhile workbook that finds the right balance. I've definitely worked hard, so I'll let you judge how worthwhile it is. My only request is that you give it an honest effort first—not because I deserve it, but rather because *you* deserve it.

2. Executive Functions Explain It All

There's a lot of good information out there about time management, organization, to-do lists, procrastination, remembering things better, etc. for folks with ADHD. Those are important topics because they affect how you live your day to day life. In this workbook I've decided to get to the root of it all—the executive functions that are responsible for those ADHD struggles—so that you can apply those strategies more effectively. By focusing on the executive functions, you're more likely to choose the most effective strategies and apply them more consistently. As you know too well, creating strategies is easy—the magic is in sticking with them.

3. Jump Around!

The good news is that you don't have to start on page one and read diligently through to the end. Feel free to jump around. The material in Section I provides some foundation knowledge to help you with the chapters in Section II, where the real exercises are. I would encourage you to read Section I first and do those exercises, but you don't necessarily have to if you feel that you know this material well already.

INTRODUCTION

EXECUTIVE FUNCTIONS EXPLAIN IT ALL

ADHD involves far more than merely not enough attention or too much hyperactivity. It affects many aspects of how you process information and manage the demands in your life and not just in the ways that are so obvious in a classroom. If only ADHD disappeared when you walked out of school at 3:00 or graduated.

Decades of research has taught us that the symptoms of ADHD are really the outcome of certain information-processing weaknesses. Specifically, ADHD involves weaknesses in a certain set of skills called the *executive functions.* The executive functions are our highest-level brain processes that enable us to navigate and make good decisions in a complex world. This is especially important as adults, when we're expected to handle our own responsibilities. Rather than respond automatically and thoughtlessly to whatever the environment throws at us (like amoebas do), we use our executive functions to modify our own thinking and behaviors in order to make the most of opportunities in both the short and long term. The executive functions enable us to see beyond the current moment by bringing back the lessons from the past and bringing forward the goals of the future to better guide our behavior in the present. Executive functions enable us to resist distractions, temptations, and the most obvious aspects of a situation in order to consider and go for the greater gain.

If you understand how the executive functions operate, everything else about ADHD makes perfect sense. The executive functions explain what makes ADHD *ADHD* and why it is different from everything else. Other conditions such as Aspergers syndrome or bipolar disorder have a different pattern of executive function strengths and weaknesses than ADHD does. The executive functions explain:

- why people with ADHD tend to have certain symptoms and struggles, but not others;

- why certain time-management and organizational strategies tend to work well for people with ADHD, whereas others don't; and

- why some treatments are effective for ADHD, whereas others aren't.

Most importantly, this unifying framework explains why your past looks the way it does and offers real promise for making your future look better.

This foundation means that you don't need to reinvent the wheel every time you're faced with a new challenge, since you already know how your brain tends to operate. This makes life much easier.

The Executive Functions Have Social Implications

As you will see in this workbook, the executive functions give rise to all sorts of important abilities. And as you probably know far too well, a significant price is paid by people who are weak in these various skills. Life as an adult in this society is complicated, so those who have weak executive functions will struggle and stand out. They will have trouble managing all the details of life and making "responsible" choices (i.e., ones that benefit the future more than the present). Many adults with untreated ADHD are seen as irresponsible or immature because they tend to react too much in the moment and lose sight of the bigger picture. Society expects and forgives this of children, but not of adults. As a result of these difficulties with managing the thousand and one details of daily life, people with ADHD spend a lot of time scrambling to hold it all together and prevent disaster. It takes a lot more energy to put out fires than to prevent them. This reactive lifestyle is much more stressful than the one led by many adults without ADHD.

We expect adults to be able to show self-control and not need as much direction from others. Because people with ADHD struggle with making themselves do the right thing at the right time, parents and romantic partners often step in to provide these executive functions to keep their loved one from going too far off the rails—for example, by reminding her about upcoming appointments, organizing her stuff, or stopping impulsive purchases. Alternatively, she may find tools that can do the job for her—for example, setting up automatic debits to eliminate having to remember to send out the bills or using a smartphone to remind her of upcoming meetings.

Fallout from Executive Function Weaknesses

The executive function weaknesses involved in ADHD lead to the symptoms that you know so well, like distractibility, forgetfulness, or impulsivity. The information-processing functions that underlie ADHD cause the symptoms, so by talking about the executive functions we're getting to the root of the problem.

I've created Figure A to illustrate the complex way that executive function weaknesses affect someone's ability to manage obligations, how they cope with the continued setbacks, and the ultimate effect on their self-esteem. I call it The Dominoes Keep Falling.

FIGURE A: The dominoes keep falling.

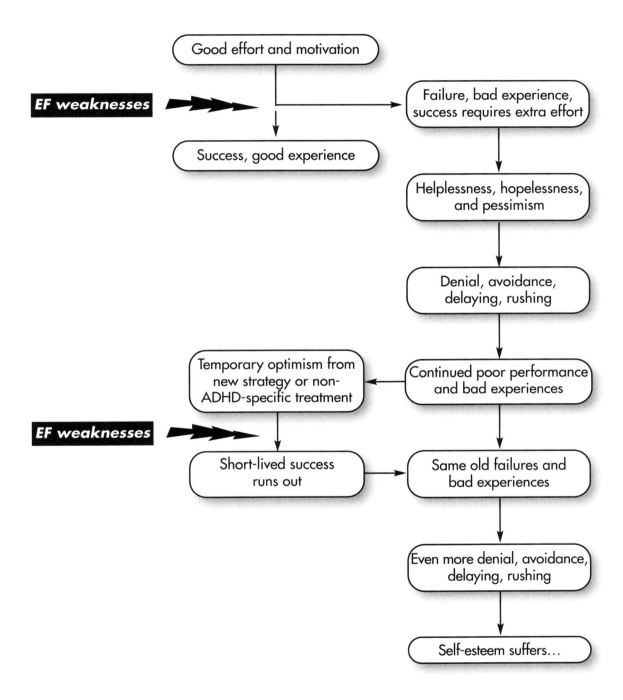

I will talk about this process, as well as how to overcome it, in more detail in the chapters in Section I. In Section II we'll go further sinto the details about how to be more effective and create a better life for yourself, as Figure B illustrates (on the next page).

It Does Get Better

As bleak as Figure A may look, there is hope. Whereas prior strategies and treatments may not have been helpful enough, applying strategies designed for ADHD is much more likely to give you the results you've been looking for, as you can see in Figure B. I call this The Game Changer.

FIGURE B: The game changer.

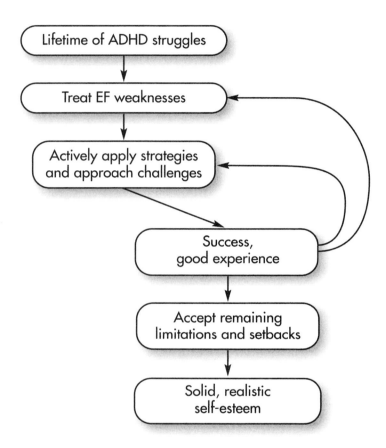

There are three ways to change your performance:

1. Improve your abilities by giving your brain what it needs to function at its best by taking appropriate medication and/or by using Cogmed Working Memory Training (see Chapter 2: Peak Mental Performance).

2. Actively approach (rather than avoid) challenges with better strategies that are based in executive functions (which is what most of this workbook is about, especially in Section II).

3. Alter the situation so the demands better fit your abilities (we will also talk about this throughout the workbook).

So jump into this, and let's see where it takes you!

Section I
SETTING THE STAGE

WE LIVE IN A COMPLICATED WORLD

You don't have to have ADHD to feel like you have ADHD. The world has become so distracting that everyone is working much harder to stay focused on what's most important while trying to ignore what's most stimulating or interesting. We also have many more belongings that need to be dealt with, shuffled about, and worked around. We also have far more opportunities in easy access to tempt our impulsivity. Many of the developments of the last decades are positive, but there are also aspects that stretch our brains' information-processing abilities to their limits. Some people in particular will feel more easily and frequently overwhelmed by the information overload.

For all of us, the challenge is to do the right thing, at the right time, most of the time. Not sometimes—most of the time. In order to do this, we need to filter out extraneous stimuli and thoughts (a.k.a. distractions) and figure out what is most important in that moment. This requires us to consider:

- Lessons from the past (e.g., How did this work out last time? What worked before?)

- The present circumstances and what our available options are

- Future goals and the balance between short- and long-term gains

Unfortunately, the most important thoughts, tasks, and items aren't always the stickiest. They don't necessarily grab our attention the hardest. Often it's quite the contrary—the distractions are distracting because they pull our attention harder than the more important items, which is kind of the definition of a distraction. (This makes sense—unimportant things that don't grab our attention are just kind of invisible and are ignored without any real effort.)

Part of what makes it so hard to figure out and then do the most important tasks is that we usually need to decide among several competing tasks, all of which have merit. In addition, life keeps evolving as the minutes tick by, so what was a great plan at one moment may change very quickly when something else comes up. Life is interruptions.

Knowing Is Easier than Doing

I sometimes say that ADHD is a disorder of actualizing good intentions. People with ADHD usually know what the right thing to do is but don't do it as consistently as they or anyone else would want. Because they already know what they should be doing, guilt-inducing lectures are rarely helpful since they don't tell people with ADHD anything new. (Even the opinion that they should feel bad about themselves is hardly a novel concept.) Therefore what guilt-inducing lectures do best is make people with ADHD feel bad and/or become angry, which is probably not the intended goal.

What the executive functions do is help us sort through this distracting, tempting world we live in so that we can decide what is the best thing to do next and then actually do it. In other words, they help us do what we know.

CHAPTER 1

A BRIEF OVERVIEW OF THE EXECUTIVE FUNCTIONS

Different researchers have created somewhat different lists of executive functions. I've found that Russell Barkley's *response inhibition theory* is the most thorough and useful of these, so the executive functions theory that I talk about in this workbook is an outgrowth of his work. His theory is incredibly detailed and impressive but contains far more information than you need to know to manage your day to day life. So I've pulled out the aspects that are most useful for your daily life—the parts that not only explain why some things are so hard for you but also set the stage for the effective strategies that we will discuss.

The Executive Functions Develop Over Time

The development of the executive functions is part of the normal process of brain maturation. As the neurons grow and make connections through our brains we develop all sorts of abilities, from crawling to speaking to thinking about abstract concepts. Generally speaking, adults have more developed abilities than children do because our brains continue to mature into our thirties.

As with most of development, this process is guided by a combination of genetics and environmental exposure. Our genes give us a range of possibilities, and then experience shapes that genetic expression. In the case of ADHD, there is a lot of genetics going on. It is one of the most heritable of all the mental health conditions. Just as there are other abilities that run in families (like being a good athlete or having an ear for music), so too are there genes that affect the neurons involved in the executive functions and ADHD.

So your ADHD isn't the result of your parents not doing a good enough job—and there isn't much that your parents could have done differently to reduce your ADHD symptoms. When it comes to your ADHD, you can only blame your parents for your genes, but you may want to avoid that line of argument if you have kids of your own.

Summaries of the Executive Functions

I have provided brief summaries of each of the executive functions that we will cover in this workbook. Hopefully this makes these sometimes amorphous concepts feel more tangible and more easily relatable to your day to day life. We're going to get very practical in the exercises, but it helps to start with a solid understanding of the theory.

Working Memory: The Brain's RAM (Chapter 6) We use working memory constantly to hold information in mind as we remember what just happened, relate it to long-term memories, and think ahead into the future. Working memory and attention work very closely together, as working memory holds what we are attending to. People with ADHD tend to have blinky working memories, which leads to a variety of problems in their daily lives.

Sense of Time: It Can't Be 5:00 Already! (Chapter 7) People with ADHD have difficulty monitoring the passage of time and planning accordingly, a skill that's really important in today's busy world. As a result, they tend to spend too long on some activities and not plan enough time for others. This contributes to their well-known problems with time-management and getting places on time.

Remembering to Remember: It's All About Timing (Chapter 8) In our busy lives we all have dozens of little (and not so little) things to remember to do over the course of a day, such as phone calls and appointments or returning to something after an interruption. People with ADHD have great difficulty reminding themselves of these tasks at the right time, often forgetting completely or remembering only when it's too late.

Emotional Self-Control: Having Feelings Without Acting on Them (Chapter 9) People with ADHD tend to feel and express their feelings more strongly than others do and are more influenced by their feelings than other people are. This then affects their ability to see beyond their emotions in the moment and to take others' perspectives into account.

Self-Activation: Starting Then Finishing (Chapter 10) Everybody has to use a certain amount of force of will to get going on boring tasks, but people with ADHD have a much steeper hill to climb. As a result, they tend to procrastinate until the pressure of a looming deadline forces them into action.

Hindsight and Forethought: Using the Past and Future to Guide the Present (Chapter 11) We use the lessons from past experiences to make better choices the next time around. We also think ahead about the likely outcomes of various actions in order to choose the plan with the best odds of success. People with ADHD tend to react too quickly in the moment and therefore don't make the time to remember the past or think about the future, so they're more likely to make less optimal choices.

Although we can intentionally choose to approach situations in certain ways, many of the executive functions operate without conscious awareness, like breathing. If you watch little kids talking themselves through a difficult task, they are sort of verbalizing their executive functions—for example, softly repeating to themselves what they are supposed to do or giving themselves pointers along the way. Eventually it becomes automatic and we don't have to think about it as much, but we may still find that we sometimes become very intentional about using our executive functions in challenging situations.

Even though I talk about specific executive functions, keep in mind that they interact constantly and that the lines between them can be pretty blurry. Don't get hung up on exactly which executive function is at work in any specific situation. The goal in this workbook is to make it understandable and applicable in your daily life, which sometimes means simplifying a little.

Response Inhibition: It Starts with Stopping

The funny thing about executive functions is that people with ADHD use them really well—except when they don't. In fact, this inconsistency is a hallmark of ADHD (if someone has consistent struggles, then the culprit is probably something other than ADHD). So how do we explain that people with ADHD sometimes perform really well, yet at other times make really simple mistakes?

This is where Barkley's response inhibition theory comes in. Unlike simpler life forms that respond automatically to stimuli from the environment, humans are able to hold back an automatic response to the world around them (as well as their internal world of thoughts and feelings). This crucial ability to stop creates a pause that allows them to think through the various response options and then choose the best one. This usually happens in a split second. An example is almost subconsciously deciding to ignore the sound of someone dropping a pen while you're working at your computer (i.e., not getting distracted) or holding your thought to what someone is saying until she finishes talking (i.e., not impulsively interrupting).

The key to successful decision making is that tiny little pause, because it gives the executive functions time to do their thing. The executive functions live in that little space between stimulus and response. People with ADHD have difficulty stopping long enough to create this pause, so they don't use their executive functions as reliably or effectively as others do. As a result, they get distracted, forget things, leap without looking, etc.—the symptoms of ADHD you know so well.

This explains why people with ADHD don't always do what they know they should. Because they have trouble creating that pause that gives them time to make a well-considered decision, they're more vulnerable to being influenced by whatever is going on around them. They have trouble filtering out external and internal stimuli, so they react to the "wrong" thing. An example is answering the phone and getting into a lengthy conversation rather than getting ready to leave the house on time. This can look like bad judgment, but what really happens is that these other stimuli have too big an impact on the ADHD person's decision making, so a less-than-optimal choice is made. It isn't bad judgment because, in these knee-jerk reactions, they didn't stop long enough to actually judge. This is why those dreaded questions of "why did/didn't you… lead to such unconvincing answers along the lines of "I don't know. I just didn't think of it," which is actually pretty accurate. Their brains didn't stop long enough to get a chance to think about it.

Because people with ADHD's difficulties with response inhibition tend to make them so vulnerable to being overly influenced by external and internal stimuli, many of the strategies to help them be more effective focus on increasing the strength of the desired stimuli or decreasing the strength of less desired stimuli so that they do the right thing in that moment. For example, a beeping alarm that tells the person to leave for a meeting overrides the focus on what else she was doing.

Medications (as well as Cogmed Working Memory Training and possibly neurofeedback) work directly by increasing the brain's ability to create that delay, thereby reversing the fallout that comes from an insufficient delay. This is also why admonitions to "just try harder" don't work—they ignore the fundamental problem that people with ADHD have trouble creating that moment of pause to try harder in. It's like telling someone who needs glasses that she just needs to try harder to see. It's a problem of ability, not desire. The confusing part is that people with ADHD usually have the ability to do the actual task (like pay the bills) but aren't as strong at the fundamental ability of creating that pause, so they don't get to the actual task.

As we talk at length about the executive functions and run through the exercises in Section II remember this delay, because this is the tripping point for many executive-functioning malfunctions. Therefore, the strategies that work well are the ones that take this into account.

Neurology and Psychology

I tend to make a somewhat artificial distinction between behaviors that are neurologically driven and those that are psychologically driven. We can't fully separate them out, but there are times when it's useful to think about these two separate contributions. Much of ADHD is neurological, but a lifetime of living with ADHD creates a whole lot of psychology.

When it comes to the executive functions, I tend to think of working memory, sense of time, and prospective memory as more purely neurological, with less of a psychological influence. Our psychological state may have some effect on how we use these executive functions, but they mostly operate without our conscious awareness.

However, emotional self-control, self-activation, and hindsight and forethought have more psychology interwoven into the neurological functioning. For example, if you feel like you always get the short end of the stick from your family, you're less likely to exhibit good emotional control when something comes up with them.

So things get more complicated with those executive functions. If you feel like you're doing pretty well on the first three executive functions but struggling a lot more with the next three, you may want to spend some extra time on Chapter 3: Reality-Based Motivation and/or Chapter 4: Work as a Team. This is especially the case if your struggles tend to show up more with some people than others or more in some situations than others.

If you feel like you have some pretty good strategies in place but things just aren't rolling for you, it may even be worth meeting with a therapist to figure out some things. I'm definitely not suggesting that therapy will cure the core features of ADHD, but it can be good for the fallout. Just make sure that you find someone who is pretty knowledgeable about ADHD in adults. I know, it can take some real looking to find someone who knows this stuff, but it's worth it if you do.

CHAPTER 2

PEAK MENTAL PERFORMANCE: MAKE THE MOST OF WHAT YOU'VE GOT

There are certain things you can do to get the best performance out of your brain and its executive functions. Some of these aren't treatments for ADHD, but are just good advice for everyone. Some of them are treatments specifically targeted for ADHD.

Your Best Brain

Your brain is an incredibly complex machine that can do phenomenal things. Like any machine, its performance depends on how you treat it. The choices you make will affect whether your brain performs at its best. As of this moment in time, there is no cure for ADHD (and nothing promising on the horizon), so it's more a matter of making the most of what you have so that you can bring your best abilities to life's challenges. This means not only the brain functions that might be affected by ADHD, but also everything else that your brain does.

You can get the most out of your brain by treating it well. This includes:

- *Good mental health.* Anxiety and depression sap our ability to solve problems efficiently, as well as our enjoyment of life, so it's important to treat any mental health concerns.

- *Good physical health.* Our brain's performance is affected by our general health. So take care of yourself, get those aches and pains checked out, and see your doctor regularly.

- *Sleep.* Our brains need sleep to recharge. They function best when we consistently get enough sleep.

- *Manage stress.* Although a little stress can bring out our best performance, too much stress hurts our performance because we lose our ability to do complex problem solving.

- *Good nutrition.* Our brains rely on quality fuel to do their work. They do best with a balanced diet that is neither lacking some nutrients nor getting overloaded by others.

- *Moderate alcohol use and minimal drug use.* Casual drinking has tolerable effects on your brain's performance and is therefore an acceptable vice. Other recreational drug use, especially if frequent, probably crosses that line where the costs outweigh the gains.

- *Regular exercise.* In addition to the well-known benefits on physical health, there is research supporting the benefits of regular exercise on mood, attention, memory, and learning.

I doubt you were terribly surprised by any of the items in this bullet list. Of course, the real trick is to actually follow all this good advice. (I call these items the New Year's resolutions stuff because so many people vow to work on them every January.) Just to make matters worse, the inconsistency that is inherent in ADHD makes it all the harder to follow these good habits. So I'm not going to give you the obvious (but pointless) advice to just try harder to do all of the above, because you've already heard it. At this point, this list is merely something to keep in mind and to work towards as you move through the workbook. In fact, we can measure your success in managing your ADHD by how well you're doing with the items on this list.

Just to get some perspective on this, let's look at how you've managed these items over time. In the table below, mark down the time in your life when you handled them the best, the worst, and how you're doing now. Mark from 1-10 (1 = poorly, 10 = excellent) how well you were managing the various items in the table and then how effectively you were handling your life overall. What I expect is that your overall effectiveness will be pretty similar to how well you were managing these lifestyle matters.

I've also included a column to mark down your goal of where you would like to get this. It would be great if you could get to a point where you're consistently rating yourself a 9 or 10 on each of these, but nobody's life is that idyllic. Also, some people are more sensitive to less than ideal conditions, whereas others are less affected. For example, some people are really affected by not getting enough sleep, whereas others do pretty well even with little sleep. Our goal here is to get you to a point where overall you're doing pretty well (or at least better than before), so don't feel like you're falling short if you rate yourself less than a 9.

Finally, I've also given you a couple columns to use in the future to track your progress over time.

	Best time	Worst time	Now	Goal	Future 1	Future 2
Date						
Mental health						
Physical health						
Sleep						
Stress						
Diet						
Alcohol/drugs						
Exercise						
Overall effectiveness						

A Vicious Cycle (Actually Two)

People with weak executive functions tend to live a life with too much chaos, disorganization, and last minute scrambling. This is the direct fallout of their difficulties with consistently managing all the details of their life and fighting to keep important details from falling through the cracks. Unfortunately, the chaos that results from their executive function weaknesses increases the burden on their executive functions so they struggle even more and fall further behind.

For example, if you tend to be forgetful you're more likely to put the bills down somewhere and then forget where you put them—or even that they came in the mail. If you have a lot of other things lying around the bills quickly get swallowed up into the mess and disappear from view, so it makes it even easier to forget about the bills because they are out of sight and out of mind. The bills then add to the amount of stuff that is spread around the house, which makes it harder to find other things. In this case, forgetfulness contributes to disorganization, which contributes to further forgetfulness. Round and round you go.

FIGURE C: The skills cycle.

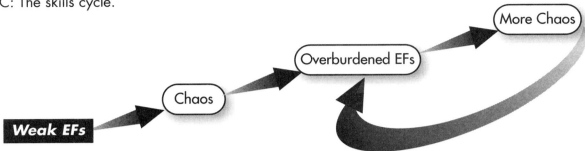

It can all get rather depressing. Attempts to get it all together (to get organized, to be on time, to remember to do things, etc.) lead to temporary successes at best. It's easy to feel hopeless and give up, or at least settle for living life a couple steps ahead of the avalanche. You still don't enjoy it, but it feels better than continuing to try to get it together, only to fail again. Failure leads to hopelessness, which leads to giving up, which leads to more failures. This emotional reaction becomes another vicious cycle.

FIGURE D: The emotional cycle.

Fortunately, there is good reason for hope. By understanding your executive functions and the strategies that will work best with your brain's way of processing information, you're much more likely to create some lasting successes. The reason why so many of your past attempts may not have worked is that they weren't based in executive functions. Unless you take your ADHD and executive functions into account, you'll be shooting in the dark when it comes to finding effective strategies. This workbook offers some good reasons for optimism that things can be better—not just wishful thinking, but real reasons. We'll talk more about realistic motivation in the next chapter and how to bring forth your best efforts.

Some Treatments Help

As problematic as undiagnosed ADHD can be, the good news is that life can be much different after getting diagnosed and starting an effective treatment regimen. Your life may never be all roses and sunshine, but it can be much better than it had been. We can't change your past, but there is something to be said for present successes vindicating past failures. Or, to put it another way, living well is the best revenge.

Based on the research, as well as clinical experience, we can say that these treatments will directly improve your executive functions:

- *Medication.* Medication increases activity in the parts of your brain involved in response inhibition, which leads to improvements in certain executive functions (see Response Inhibition in Chapter 1). This causes your brain to function more like the brains of people who don't have ADHD.

- *Cogmed Working Memory Training.* This computerized attention training program strengthens working memory (one of the core executive functions) that leads to improved performance in other executive functions.

- *Neurofeedback.* The research is still mixed about the benefits of neurofeedback, so we can't say for certain that it works, but if it does, then it would lead to some improvements in executive functioning.

There is a saying that pills don't teach skills (that's what the rest of this workbook is for), but they do lay a solid foundation for the other good work you do. Same for Cogmed Working Memory Training and perhaps neurofeedback. They give you a little more time to think through your options before responding and enable you to be more consistent. This makes it easier to apply all those good intentions, as well as the strategies from this workbook, so that you're more likely to do the right thing at the right time.

I wrote about all of this at length in my book *More Attention, Less Deficit: Success Strategies for Adults with ADHD*, so you can check that out for more information.

Externalized Executive Functions

Externalized executive functions refers to using tools to do what it is difficult for your brain to do or at least to do consistently. For example, if you are bad at keeping track of time, you can set an alarm on your phone for when it's time to leave for a meeting. Or ask someone else to remind you. Instead of relying on your internal executive functions, you outsource the job to something else that is more reliable. (OK, this isn't technically a treatment, but it does help you make the most of your existing executive functions and abilities.)

We do this sort of thing all the time—like when we write out a shopping list or put up a Post-It note to remind us of something. In this context, we're talking about a specific habit to use external supports to supplement internal abilities in order to assist the other executive functions to do their best. I sprinkle the use of tools and technology throughout the workbook, but feel free to come up with your own tools that help you be more effective.

CHAPTER 3

REALITY-BASED MOTIVATION

Too many self-help books seem to promise too much, which is a set-up for disappointment when you inevitably fall short. I prefer to promise a realistic amount so that you can give yourself credit for the progress that you do make (and maybe even surprise yourself). Most of this workbook will contain exercises for you to do and strategies for you to try. It's important that you give them good effort if you're to see any changes in your life. I want you to be motivated to try these strategies and continue practicing them because you feel like it might actually help. Without this motivation, my strategies and your abilities won't get you much. So let's talk in this chapter about how to keep that motivation running strong so that you can bring your best effort to this endeavor.

Let's begin by taking a look at where you are now by rating these questions below from 1-10 (1 = none, 10 = a lot).

- How likely do you think it is that you will be able to make some noticeable improvements in your executive functioning? ____

- How much would this affect your overall functioning in your day to day life? ____

- How much happier would you be? ____

- How much happier would the people around you be? ____

- How motivated are you to give this the work it requires? ____

It's OK if you are skeptical about how much progress can be made here. When it comes to these matters, skepticism is often warranted. I just want you to have enough optimism that you're willing to give it a fair shot. Of course, if you had no hope of improvement you wouldn't even be reading this, so I can assume that you want your life to be better and think you have at least some chance of making that happen.

I want you to decide how much effort to put in based on an accurate appraisal of the likelihood of success. Although we look to our pasts to inform our decisions in the present, sometimes we need to let go of that past, look to see what's different this time, and cross our fingers. Whereas in the past it might have felt that you struggled regardless of how much effort you put in or that hard work gave you only temporary successes, perhaps this time can be different, and you will be able to create more lasting progress. There's only one way to find out—take a deep breath and see what you can do.

We Can Tilt the Odds of Success

It's unreasonable to expect different outcomes from the same efforts, but that's the great news about ADHD—it responds very well to treatment and to adapted strategies. As I've said before, ADHD is worst before you know it is what you're dealing with. Once you know that it's ADHD it becomes a fair fight, and you have a competent chance of winning. Getting diagnosed is a total game changer because it completely changes the strategies you will use and the odds of being successful.

Treatment makes your situation better in two ways. First, it truly helps you be more effective and consistent so that you legitimately have more to feel good about in your life. It isn't just pretty but empty words about everyone being special while you continue to struggle to keep the chaos at bay. Second and related to this, the current successes that treatment brings also make it easier to leave those old setbacks and failures in the past so you can feel better about yourself now. This makes it easier to give current challenges your best effort so they are even more likely to work out well. Just as failures often lead to more failures, each success can also feed the next success.

Permanent or Changeable?

Given the track record that often comes with undiagnosed and untreated ADHD, it's easy (and even pretty smart) to be skeptical about each new strategy you come across. It's easy to believe that not much will change. You've experienced too many otherwise reasonable strategies that wound up ultimately falling flat, and you're back where you started.

Psychologists who study depression have found that depressed people tend to see their situation as unchangeable. After all, a bad and unchanging situation is pretty depressing. The good news is that seeing at least some of the negatives in your situation as changeable gives you reason not only to feel better, but also to try some new strategies.

This workbook is full of new strategies that are much more likely to be helpful than the generic advice you've gotten over the years. I'm not going to over-promise and say that this workbook will change your entire life, but I do have faith that in combination with your good efforts, you will see noticeable and worthwhile improvements. I ask you to at least consider the possibility that the struggles that seemed so permanent before might actually be changeable, at least if you approach them differently.

Build Strong Self-Esteem

Even though we all enjoy hearing other people say nice things about us, good self-esteem comes most from real successes, that is, facing challenges, testing ourselves, and coming out victorious. This doesn't mean getting a 100 on every test, but rather accomplishing whatever goal we had set for ourselves. Sometimes success just means passing the test. This is especially true if you feel like you had to work harder for those successes. Rather than being a cut against you, this extra effort can actually give you more to feel good about yourself.

Self-esteem comes from feeling good at the things that matter to us while being able to let go of the things that we aren't good at. For example, I'm a pretty bad cook, but I don't really care. It isn't important to me. Fortunately, I do feel good about being a skilled therapist, diligent husband, and caring father, so I get my self-esteem there.

We get our self-esteem from three places:

- *Traits*. These are enduring qualities about you, such as generosity, intelligence, attractiveness, athletic, funny, charming, etc. Although you may intentionally work to improve some of these, they are a part of who you are.

- *Skills*. These are the abilities you possess, such as being a good batter, knowing how to play an instrument, being an engaging public speaker, or being good at talking with kids. Obviously these abilities probably line up with traits that you have a natural gift for, but these are skills that you have learned and probably practiced.

- *Experiences*. Over the course of your life you've had lots of experiences that have taught you about yourself and also the world around you. For example, the "A" you got on your sixth grade science project showed you that you can do well in school when it's something interesting and you work hard at it. Or the meeting you were in last week where a problem came up but you could think on your feet because you had prepared for the meeting ahead of time and knew your stuff.

Our experiences teach us how our traits and skills stack up against others. We also look to what people say about us—are we getting compliments or criticism? Based on all this information we create a picture of ourselves. Of course, it isn't a simple matter of accounting, where you total up all the compliments and then subtract the criticism to come up with your self-esteem. We also interpret all the events that go on around us—for example, a criticism from a boss who is nasty to everyone just confirms that the boss is a jerk, but probably doesn't teach us much about ourselves or our performance.

Unfortunately, ADHD makes it easy to misinterpret your actions and what they mean about your traits and skills. For example, repeatedly forgetting about meetings could be interpreted to mean that you're irresponsible or even stupid, even if you're very diligent and intelligent. The problem here is that ADHD interferes with your ability to consistently demonstrate your abilities, so you and others will get the wrong picture of who you are. This is one of the reasons why getting diagnosed can be so liberating. It takes away the interpretations of irresponsibility or stupidity and replaces them with the idea that you have a brain-based condition that makes it hard for you to track time or remember to do things. Much better.

Which brings us to the idea that good self-esteem doesn't mean that you like everything about yourself. Everybody has things about themselves that they wish were different. Everybody has experiences where they wish they had acted differently. Those with good self-esteem are able to accept those parts of themselves and balance them out with their more positive qualities to create a complete and accurate picture of themselves that they can feel good about overall.

I will cover the topic of self-esteem at length in my next book, *The ADHD Self-Esteem Workbook*.

Approach Challenges

The people who are most successful in life are the ones who approach challenges, rather than avoid them. This means trying new things, as well as sticking with something after a setback. As the old saying goes, if at first you don't succeed, try, try again. This doesn't mean that you won't have times when you feel anxious, frustrated, annoyed, or confused, because it's totally normal to have those feelings. In fact, if you rarely feel any of these, you're probably playing it too safe (which is really boring). Courage isn't the absence of fear, courage is doing something despite your fears—or doubts, frustration, annoyance, confusion…

This doesn't mean doggedly persisting at something past the point of good judgment, because that can cause other problems. It's a matter of finding the right balance of knowing when to stick with something versus when it's better to change tactics or even walk away.

Unfortunately, after too many experiences where things didn't work out well, despite their best efforts, lots of people with ADHD become pessimistic or hopeless and don't apply themselves fully. They sometimes avoid challenges entirely (e.g., "there's no point going back to college because I'll just fail out again") or they give something insufficient effort (e.g., quickly throwing together a cover letter and resume when applying for a better job). Unfortunately, this then becomes a self-fulfilling prophecy. In the first case of avoiding a challenge entirely, the person never gets a chance to see if it could work out or to learn something from the experience so that they are better off for the next situation. In the second case of cutting corners, the less than polished job application makes it unlikely that they will get the job. Each of these reinforces the idea that things won't get better, so don't bother trying.

To succeed you must be willing to fail. Nobody likes to fall short, but it's hard to get anywhere in life without taking some chances. One way to make it easier to take those chances is to see the important lessons that can come from both successes and failures.

What Lies Are You Telling Yourself?

We all tell ourselves little lies occasionally in order to make the day go smoother, justify a shortcut, or keep the guilt at bay. This is common, but not always helpful. We all tend to have certain favorite lies that we use most (e.g., fast food isn't that unhealthy, and besides, I just don't have time to eat otherwise). Given that you're going to be working on some important but sometimes difficult habit changes, it's worth keeping in mind the lies that you tend to use to get yourself out of doing the things that you don't really feel like doing. This will help you stay honest with yourself.

Write out your favorite lies and how you know when you're trying to con yourself.

Lie	How I know When It's Fake
I'll have more energy to work on that tomorrow	*I just don't want to do it now*

_____   _____
_____   _____
_____   _____
_____   _____
_____   _____
_____   _____
_____   _____
_____   _____
_____   _____

Approach Challenges Like a Scientist

Scientists doing research start out with a theory, run some experiments, and then examine the results. Sometimes they hit the bullseye on the first shot; usually they don't. So they analyze the results for clues about what to try next, then they repeat this process until they do hit the bullseye.

Just as in science, few real accomplishments in life are achieved on the first effort, from learning to ride a bike to creating a good romantic relationship. Most challenges in life are complicated and take some time to figure out and fine-tune your approach. One way to make failure less daunting, and thereby make success more likely, is to look at failures as learning opportunities: "Hmm, that didn't work. Let's try to figure out why." If you can learn some good lessons, then that failure is a success because it has moved you forward. You are one step closer to getting it right.

To illustrate this, let's take a look at some of the failures (both big and small) you've had and the valuable lessons that you learned from them that set you up for future success.

Failure _Thanksgiving dinner was ready 3 hours late_____

Lessons learned _____don't try new recipes on the big day_____
_(no matter how good they look)_____

Future benefit _____more likely to stick with the tried and true, rather
than trying something new and flashy, when it really matters___

Failure _____

Lessons learned _____

_____

Future benefit _____

_____

Failure _____

Lessons learned _____

_____

Future benefit _____

_____

Failure _____

Lessons learned _____

_____

Future benefit _____

_____

Failure _____

Lessons learned _____

_____

Future benefit _____

_____

It might have been nice to skip those initial failures, but looking at what you just wrote, is it realistic to think that you could have known all of this before you tried it? Or did you have to go through this process to figure out some things?

So just as we've seen here, one of the key ingredients of success is being willing to keep trying. That persistence also gives you additional opportunities to practice and sharpen your skills.

The Magic Threshold

It would be great if we could turn all of our weaknesses into strengths, but it's more realistic to expect some partial improvement. For example, it would be great if you were never late again, but that would be really hard to pull off even if you didn't have ADHD. It's probably better to focus on being less late, less often. This is much more doable and therefore makes it easier to maintain motivation. If you set the bar too high you'll quickly get discouraged and give up, so you won't make even partial progress. By giving yourself credit for the successes that you are having, you're more likely to keep trying. Remember that progress is a process that will take some time. After all, you've already figured out all the easy answers in your life, so you're now left with the challenges that will take more work.

You may also find that other people are much happier with your performance, even with only partial progress. For example, your boss may notice it a lot less if you're only late once a week instead of twice and if you go from being twenty minutes late to ten. This is what I call the magic threshold—that unspoken number under which you're doing well enough. In this example, your boss may be happy with the rest of your job performance and is willing to let your lateness slide as long as it isn't excessive. So even partial progress can lead to significant improvements in your relationships with others, as well as in how you feel about yourself.

Think for a moment about the magic thresholds that you might have discovered. What are some areas of your life where you made some partial improvement that translated into a big change in how you or others see you?

Area of Partial Progress

When I catch myself interrupting, I stop and ask the other person to continue

Corresponding Improvements

people are much less annoyed

Remember also that success is rarely a straight line. When you find yourself slipping back think for a moment about what might be causing that, then get yourself back on track with the good habits that brought you those initial successes. Although you may always need to work at some of these habits, they should get easier the longer you use them.

The Trap of Perfectionism

Some people strive for perfection as a way to ward off doubt—"If I do this perfectly, then I can feel good about myself." While there is a lot to be said for the idea of taking pride in your work, perfectionism is actually a trap where you get much less done because you spend so long polishing the final details that you never actually finish the task (or maybe even start it) and move on to other important tasks. It can be anxiety provoking to say that something is finished and therefore put it open to comment and criticism, but refusing to let something go only causes more problems by limiting your overall productivity.

What If...

Before you commit to do something, it's helpful to know what you might get from it. Our willingness to do something depends on several factors:

- *The cost.* How much effort will it take? What are the risks?

- *The gains.* What can we reasonably hope for if this does work out?

- *The odds.* How likely is this to be successful?

I can't promise you that your life will be perfect if you apply yourself to the strategies in this workbook, but I do think that you have some solid reasons to expect things to be better. You will be more consistent, more effective, more reliable, and more efficient. You will be on top of your life more, rather than feeling like your life is on top of you. So let's talk about what you could reasonably expect if you got ADHD under better control.

What goals would you pursue if you felt you could be more effective?

_____

_____

_____

_____

_____

_____

_____

_____

_____

_____

How would your life look different if you were doing better?

_____

_____

_____

_____

_____

_____

_____

_____

_____

_____

Obviously this workbook won't change everything in your life (it won't make you any taller), but if you can make some good progress on at least some of these areas, the stuff that remains may not bother you as much. You may feel happier overall and have an easier time accepting the things that haven't changed.

Checking Back In

Hopefully this chapter has helped you to see that some optimism is well founded. Let's take another look at the questions I asked you at the start of the chapter. After you fill them out, take a look at what you wrote in the beginning (no cheating!).

As before, rate these questions below from 1-10 (1 = none, 10 = a lot).

■ How likely do you think it is that you will be able to make
   some noticeable improvements in your executive functioning?   ____

■ How much would this affect your overall functioning in your day to day life?   ____

■ How much happier would you be?   ____

■ How much happier would the people around you be?   ____

■ How motivated are you to give this the work it requires?   ____

Are your answers now any different from what you wrote at the beginning of the chapter? If not, that's OK, but you may want to take another look at these last pages and reconsider your initial impressions, especially if your ratings are less than 5. I very much appreciate that it is risky to open yourself up to optimism, that you risk yet another disappointment. I take my responsibility as an author very seriously and have given you the best workbook I can so that you have the greatest likelihood of success. We're in this together!

CHAPTER 4

WORK AS A TEAM

No man is an island, even if sometimes a week alone on one sounds pretty spectacular. Our actions affect our family members and romantic partners, just as their actions affect us. We respond to their responses which are response to our responses. So it's hard to start from scratch with someone we're close to.

When one person in a couple or family has ADHD, we can kind of say that everyone else has it too. The natural human tendency to respond to others' responses makes the relationship complicated pretty quickly. The stereotypical pattern that develops is that the person who doesn't have ADHD gets frustrated with the ADHD person's inconsistency and begins to take over certain tasks. This way the non-ADHD person doesn't need to worry about things getting done, and the person with ADHD is probably pretty happy to be rid of tasks that don't cater to his strengths. This works well enough until the non-ADHD person feels overloaded and resentful.

At this point, she starts pushing the person with ADHD to do more and becomes more controlling to make sure it gets done. Obviously no one likes to be controlled, so the person with ADHD rebels. Sometimes the rebellion is right out in the open, and arguments ensue. Other times, the rebellion is more underground, where the person with ADHD covers up, minimizes problems, and even lies about what he has done. This is when the relationship really struggles, even though each response is reasonable in its way. The non-ADHD partner becomes more controlling in an effort to reduce her anxiety about the situation. The ADHD partner tries to avoid conflict and feel less claustrophobic. Unfortunately, each person drives the other's behavior, and the situation goes from bad to worse.

This tug of war is especially likely before a diagnosis is made and more effective treatment initiated. This can change the relationship pattern completely, as a shift in each partner is reinforced by a change in the other person's behavior.

If you have a romantic partner or a family member who is closely involved in your day to day life, this chapter will be a good one for you.

You're in This Together

Even though it's really easy to fall into negative momentum where each partner's behavior brings out some of the worst in the other person, it's also possible to turn that momentum around so that each person brings out more of the best in the other. It's possible for only one person to change a relationship because the other person will have to respond to the first person's changes. But relationships change faster (and usually better) if both people are willing to work on things together—for both of you.

This means being willing to let go of old behaviors, even you think that they are justified or appropriate. I have created several relationship laws. We often try to ignore the laws or convince ourselves that we don't need to follow them, which eventually leads to trouble. In happy relationships, both partners follow the laws, even if they're not consciously aware of them.

- Your partner won't work harder than you do on the relationship.

- Your partner won't behave better than you do.

- Your partner won't stick with a positive change if you don't also change for the better.

- Therefore, make it easy for your partner to do his/her right things by doing your right things first/also.

If you feel stuck in your relationship, you need to try some new things. The more new things you try, the more likely you are to find something that works and to break the pattern you're stuck in. The thing is, you can't try something new unless you're willing to let go of something old first.

Couples where one or both partners have ADHD will face certain challenges that others won't (or at least as often), but every happy relationship has faced and overcome some challenges. ADHD couples will need to address certain situations more explicitly, such as balancing out fairness of who does what and negotiating the differences.

Work at It

Let's run through some exercises to help you see where your relationship is now and where you want to go with it. You may find it most helpful to write out these exercises and then discuss them. Use your written notes as a springboard for discussion.

Notice the Positives

What do you like about your partner? What does s/he do that makes you happy? On the right side, write what you think your partner likes about you and what you do that makes him/her happy.

My Partner's Positives

_____

_____

_____

_____

_____

_____

_____

_____

_____

My Positives

_____

_____

_____

_____

_____

_____

_____

_____

_____

If s/he is interested (and I hope so), have your partner do the same thing in the space below.

Non-ADHD partner: What do you like about your partner? What does s/he do that makes you happy? On the right side, write what you think your partner likes about you and what you do that makes him/her happy.

My Partner's Positives

_____
_____
_____
_____
_____
_____
_____
_____
_____

My Positives

_____
_____
_____
_____
_____
_____
_____
_____
_____

One Good Deed Deserves Another

A good relationship depends on nice gestures to smooth away the tensions that invariably develop in a busy life. Unfortunately, that busy life makes it easy to not notice our partner's good deeds, so it's worth specifically looking for them once in a while.

List the nice gestures that you have recently done for your partner and that your partner has done for you. These can be grand gestures or fleeting moments.

My Good Deeds

_____
_____
_____
_____
_____
_____
_____
_____
_____

My Partner's Good Deeds

_____
_____
_____
_____
_____
_____
_____
_____
_____

If s/he is interested (and I hope so), have your partner do the same thing in the space below.

Non-ADHD partner: List the nice gestures that you have recently done for your partner and that your partner has done for you. These can be grand gestures or fleeting moments.

My Good Deeds   My Partner's Good Deeds

_____   _____

_____   _____

_____   _____

_____   _____

_____   _____

_____   _____

_____   _____

_____   _____

_____   _____

Strive for Balance

List the chores/responsibilities that each of you tends to do on a regular basis. You may want to do this together to be sure you think of everything (or most of it).

Myself   My Partner

_____   _____

_____   _____

_____   _____

_____   _____

_____   _____

_____   _____

_____   _____

_____   _____

_____   _____

Would it be worth shifting around who does what, either for the sake of variety or to make it a fairer division of labor? If so, how?

_____

_____

_____

_____

_____

_____

_____

_____

_____

_____

Strive for Understanding

It's easy to get lost in our own perspective and lose sight of our partner's perspective.

For the ADHD partner: What do you want your partner to understand about your ADHD?

_____

_____

_____

_____

_____

_____

_____

_____

_____

For the non-ADHD partner: What do you want your partner to understand about how his/her ADHD affects you?

_____

_____

_____

_____

_____

_____

_____

_____

_____

_____

_____

Repeat the Past

We sometimes fall away from good habits and patterns, even though they used to work well in the past. It can be helpful to bring back some of those proven strategies.

Write what your partner used to do that was helpful to you that you wish s/he would do more of now. On the right, write what s/he used to do that wasn't as helpful and that you would like to see less of now.

Do More	Do Less
_____	_____
_____	_____
_____	_____
_____	_____
_____	_____
_____	_____
_____	_____
_____	_____
_____	_____
_____	_____

Look Forward

This workbook will give you a lot of exercises to try. By working together with your partner, these exercises will be more helpful and you will both be happier. How can your partner support the work that you're doing here? Of course this may change over time, but it's worth starting out with some good ideas.

Write what your partner can do more often to be helpful to you. On the right, write what s/he could do *less* often.

Do More

Do Less

_____

_____

_____

_____

_____

_____

_____

_____

_____

If s/he is interested (and I hope so), have your partner do the same thing in the space below.

Non-ADHD partner: Write what your partner can do more often to be helpful to you. On the right, write what s/he could do *less* often.

Do More

Do Less

_____

_____

_____

_____

_____

_____

_____

_____

_____

We Want Everyone to Win

The solutions that last the longest are the ones where everybody wins. This is because no one has an incentive to change it. My hope is that the process of working on the exercises in this workbook will not only help your executive functioning, but will also indirectly improve your relationship if you can learn to work together more effectively through this process. That's an ambitious statement, but I've seen couples who have risen to the challenge. There's no reason to think that you can't do it, too.

Section II
MAKE YOUR LIFE BETTER

GET DOWN TO BUSINESS

Section I set things up by helping you understand how the executive functions affect your life, your mindset, and your relationships. In Section II, we're going to dive into the exercises that will help you make the most of your executive functions. This is where things begin to get better.

A Recipe for Success

Success in most endeavors usually comes down to two things: persistence and a willingness to learn from experience. Both are important, and both are necessary.

Persistence

Most achievements of any significance require ongoing effort and a willingness to continue despite setbacks. Working on your ADHD and executive functions is no different—it's going to take some work. Like I said in the first few pages this is a workbook, and you're going to have to work at it. But good effort will be rewarded.

A Willingness to Learn from Experience

Although persistence is important, it just leads to stubbornly repeating the same mistakes if you don't pair it with a willingness to learn from what your experiences are teaching you. This means being willing to try something new to see how it goes, then applying those lessons to the next time. It also means adapting flexibly to the circumstances and using the best strategy for the situation. Try the exercises and strategies in this workbook, even if they don't initially feel natural. You may find that they become more familiar with practice, especially once you start getting some benefit in your day to day life.

Where to Begin?

Each chapter in this section tends to build on the chapters that came before it, so it's probably best to work through them in order. However, you may find that you have a more pressing need or desire to work on one of the later chapters first. That's OK, too. You can use the following table to help you decide what area you want to work on first.

If you want to work on...	Then start with chapter...
Holding information in mind better without getting distracted or forgetting it	6: Working Memory
Managing your time better	7: Sense of Time
Remembering what you need to do and doing the right things at the right times	8: Prospective Memory
Managing your emotions more effectively so you are less driven by what you feel in the moment	9: Emotional Self-Control
Starting and finishing boring tasks before the last minute	10: Self-Activation
Making wiser choices and thinking more about your long-term goals and the bigger picture	11: Hindsight & Forethought

If you do decide to skip ahead to a later chapter, you will probably benefit from doing Chapter 5: Response Inhibition first. Because the executive functions are based on our ability to create a gap between stimulus and response, it's response inhibition that makes them possible.

Different Areas, Same Exercises

I repeat the same exercises in the six executive function chapters. I do this for three important reasons.

- You may not do the chapters in order, so I don't want you to miss out on some important concepts.

- You will have an easier time with later chapters if you're already familiar with the exercises.

- Each time you go through the exercises, you may learn something new.

So if you'll pardon the repetition, I think it will be worth your time.

CHAPTER 5

RESPONSE INHIBITION: IT STARTS WITH STOPPING

As we discussed in Chapter 1: A Brief Overview of the Executive Functions, we depend on the ability to create a pause between stimulus and response in order to have a moment to apply our executive functions. Because people with ADHD don't pause as often or as long, they too often don't apply their executive functions as reliably or effectively. As a result, they tend to be overly influenced by whatever is going on in the moment or the more intense aspects of the situation. When they pause for a moment they may instead focus on and respond to the less obvious aspects.

Fundamental Strategies Improve Response Inhibition

After thinking about all those lists and lists of strategies that tend to work better for folks with ADHD, it occurred to me that all those strategies essentially boil down to six basic ideas—what I call the fundamental strategies. There are two for each of the three symptom clusters of inattention, hyperactivity, and impulsivity. (Some people only have the inattentive symptoms, whereas other people also have the hyperactive and impulsive symptoms.) For the most part, the strategies that are most successful for people with ADHD will be consistent with the fundamental strategies because they take into account the difficulties with response inhibition that are inherent to ADHD.

By understanding the six fundamental strategies you will be in a better position to create your own effective ways of dealing with whatever life throws at you. You will also be able to understand why a strategy is ADHD-friendly, which makes those long lists less overwhelming because you will see that they are all just variations on six simple themes.

Fundamental Strategies for Inattention

People with ADHD have difficulty keeping their attention on the most relevant part of their environment. They tend to get pulled off by other stimuli that may be flashier but aren't as important. This could be distractions in the world around them or distractions from within their own thoughts. The goal, therefore, is to reduce the odds of getting off track and thereby increase the chances of doing the right things at the right times. We can increase the relative intensity of the important stimuli by both decreasing the strength of undesirable stimuli as well as increasing the strength of the desired ones.

We can do this by working it from both sides:

- **Reduce extraneous stimuli**. The fewer distractions that are competing for your attention, the more likely you are to stay focused where you should be. You can assist this process by reducing clutter, noise, visual stimuli, or reminders of tasks you shouldn't be engaging in, such as by turning off your phone or e-mail alert. By eliminating these sticky stimuli, you would have to make a conscious choice to get off track, as opposed to getting drawn off and stuck to a distraction before you even realize it.

■ Amplify important stimuli. The stronger and stickier the desired stimuli are, the more likely you are to notice and stay on them. So leaning your umbrella against the front door makes it stand out much more than relying on your memory to take it from the hall closet when heading off to work. Similarly, a big reminder note taped up on the wall is much more noticeable than a note written inside a schedule book. The general idea is to prevent the important stimuli from fading into the background and instead to bring them forward, front and center.

You already have some good strategies for coping with inattention that work well when you apply them. Let's see how they fit into the fundamental strategies.

List the strategies that you already use where you reduce extraneous stimuli:

Close office door when I really need to concentrate

_____

_____

_____

_____

_____

_____

_____

List the strategies that you already use where you amplify important stimuli:

Mark important parts of paper work with a highlighter

_____

_____

_____

_____

_____

_____

_____

Fundamental Strategies for Hyperactivity

You may or may not have ever been hyperactive as a child. If you had been, you're probably much less active as an adult. Much of the obvious activity will settle down, but it is often replaced with a more internal sense of restlessness. You can probably make yourself sit still for extended periods if you have to but it may take mental effort, so you would rather avoid it if possible.

Just as the two fundamental strategies for inattention are opposite sides of the same coin, so too are there two complementary strategies for coping with hyperactivity:

- *Seek out situations that allow for the safe expression of hyperactivity.* If you need to move to satisfy that internal restlessness, then look for times and places where you can. Many ADHD adults wisely select the situations they put themselves into. For example, they will watch movies at home where they can move around easily rather than feel trapped at the theater. Others may need to counterbalance the mental efforts and demands for restraint at work with more active pursuits at night and on weekends.

- *Minimize or avoid situations that require more restraint than you can muster.* There's little to be gained from putting yourself into situations that force you to do something you're bad at, at least if you can avoid it. (Sometimes you can't.) For example, someone who hates sitting still should avoid a desk job that doesn't allow frequent breaks. You may find that you have greater tolerance for repetitive or boring activities if you allow yourself some breaks, remind yourself of the benefits of doing the task, or build in a reward. It may still take some real mental effort and you may never be great at it, but it's still worth working on.

You already have some good strategies for coping with hyperactivity that work well when you apply them. Let's see how they fit into the fundamental strategies.

List the strategies that you already use where you seek out situations that allow for the safe expression of hyperactivity:

Meet friends for a walk rather than just sitting somewhere and talking

_____

_____

_____

_____

_____

_____

_____

_____

_____

List the strategies that you already use where you minimize or avoid situations that require more restraint than you can muster:

Watch movies at home, instead of the theater, so I can move around.

Fundamental Strategies for Impulsivity

I tend to define impulsivity as actions that precede conscious thought. Or more simplistically, leaping before looking. It's easy to say "Don't act impulsively," but that just doesn't work (as you undoubtedly already know). The problem is that you will have already leapt before realizing that you didn't look. Apart from inventing a time machine, you will do better if you set yourself up for success before you find yourself in certain situations. There's less to think about this way, and less willpower is needed.

Once again, we have two complementary strategies for coping with impulsivity:

■ *Create barriers to problematic actions by reducing tempting stimuli.* This is the "lead me not into temptation" approach. For example, if there are stores where you tend to spend too much money or websites where you tend to spend too much time, then don't even go there in the first place. Whatever good intentions you have going in may be quickly overcome and lost. It's much easier to not be tempted if there is no temptation. This way you don't have to rely on willpower to hold you back— willpower has a disappointing tendency to run out of steam.

■ *Set up cushions to reduce the potential damage.* Sometimes you can't remove or avoid temptations completely. However, you may still be able to find ways to minimize the potential costs of impulsive acts if you do give in. For example, if you need to go into a store where it's too easy to spend too much money, take a specific amount of cash with you and leave the credit cards at home. This way you can't spend more than planned, no matter how excited you get about something. Although there's some potential benefit from working on self-control and reminding yourself in the moment about the consequences of an impulsive act, you will probably have greater success with setting yourself up correctly beforehand.

You already have some good strategies for coping with impulsivity that work well when you apply them. Let's see how they fit into the fundamental strategies.

List the strategies that you already use where you create barriers to problematic actions by reducing tempting stimuli:

Dont' bring junk food home

_____

_____

_____

_____

_____

_____

_____

_____

List the strategies that you already use where you set up cushions to reduce the potential damage:

Set the sleep timer on the TV so it shuts off after one show

_____

_____

_____

_____

_____

_____

_____

_____

The Stage is Set

Now that we have talked about response inhibition, we're ready to get into the more specific details related to the various executive functions that make up the rest of Section II. Away we go!

CHAPTER 6

WORKING MEMORY: THE BRAIN'S RAM

What Working Memory Is

Even though we often talk of memory as if there were only one kind, we actually have many kinds of memory. People with ADHD sometimes complain that they don't remember well. (And their family members probably complain more!) This is somewhat true, but not completely. Their *long-term memory* is fine—for example, the chemical formula for water is H_2O or my third-grade teacher was Mrs. Phillips. Although folks with ADHD may get distracted at times when trying to remember this information, their long-term memories actually work well.

Where they run into trouble is in getting information *into* that long-term memory. If something never gets into long-term memory then there is nothing there to remember, so it isn't really a memory problem at that point. Where things break down is in the *working memory*, which is the part of memory that holds information in the moment as it is being processed and then either generates a response and/or tucks some information away for later. It's the part of our memory that is doing the work—it's holding information on deck and/or doing something with it. Informally, you can think of working memory as what we commonly call attention because it holds information we're paying attention to.

To use a computer analogy, long-term memory is like the hard drive, and working memory is like the RAM. The hard drive holds information for long periods of time, while the RAM takes in new information, pulls information from the hard drive, processes it all together, and then generates an output and/or writes the new information to the hard drive. The information in RAM is constantly changing, whereas the contents of the hard drive change more incrementally. By the same token, our working memory is constantly taking in information, doing something with it, and then clearing it out to make room for the next incoming information. There is a constant flow of information through our working memory where information is held only while it is being used and then gets dropped or knocked out. Our long-term memory changes much more slowly as new information is added to what we already know.

The more RAM your computer has, the more it can process at once without dropping important pieces of information (i.e., getting distracted). Having a lot of RAM in your computer allows you to continue surfing the web smoothly while the virus software scans. Given the multitude of distractions in our current lives, we all feel like we could use a little more mental RAM to keep track of it all.

We use working memory whenever we do anything that involves holding or processing two or more pieces of information. For example:

- Remembering what we read at the start of a paragraph as we read the end of the paragraph and then putting it all together

- Remembering the first part of what someone said as we listen to the last part and then making sense of it

- Transferring information from our attention into long-term memory

- Connecting a new piece of information with something from long-term memory, such as considering how a new task will fit into an existing schedule

- Keeping multi-step directions in mind, such as the next three steps in a recipe

- Holding some pieces of information while simultaneously paying attention to others, like keeping in mind that you need to do the laundry while you stop to answer a child's question

We use working memory constantly and in almost every aspect of daily life. If a person's working memory tends to blink and drop pieces of information, all sorts of problems occur, as you probably know far too well. So even if the rest of your brain works great and you are absolutely brilliant, a weak working memory will limit your ability to perform to your potential (something else you probably know too well). It will limit how much information you can get into your brain to process and then also limit how much you can generate, so it gets you on both the input and the output.

Identify Your Struggles

Good solutions begin with a clear understanding of the problem. We'll begin here by listing the ways that working memory weaknesses tend to affect someone's day to day life. You will then have some room to write other ways that your working memory affects your life. Having this all in one place will make it easier to prioritize which areas to focus on first when we get to the strategies section.

Fallout from Working Memory Weaknesses

To use a computer analogy, long-term memory is like the hard drive and working memory is like the RAM. So ADHD folks' hard drives work well, but their RAM is kind of glitchy. Just as when you try to do too many things at once on your computer and a program crashes, people with ADHD are prone to working memory dumps where something important gets pushed out by something new.

For example, your cell phone rings while you are walking back to your desk to get some information for your boss, and your attention goes to that, so your boss's request gets knocked out of your working memory. If you're lucky, some bits and pieces got recorded into your long-term memory so that you can remember it later, especially if reminded by seeing the requested paperwork sitting on your desk. (Oh right, the papers!) Other times the memory is completely gone, so even a lie detector wouldn't pick anything up when your boss asks why you didn't get her the information. (What information? You didn't ask for any information.) It's easy to get the feeling that other people enjoy making things up if you have no memory of things that others swear happened. This also makes for all sorts of fun arguments.

Weaknesses in working memory tend to create common and predictable struggles in daily life. For example:

- *Distractibility.* We use our working memory to hold in mind what we are doing and what our next steps are. We also use our working memory to hold those thoughts on deck when we're interrupted by a new stimulus or idea and then evaluate whether to stay on our original plan or switch to something new. People with ADHD are more likely to drop that original plan out of their working memories and get pulled off onto something else, even if they know better. When important pieces of information get dropped out of working memory, they don't do what they otherwise know they should do (e.g., put the milk back in the fridge before checking the weather report).

■ *Imperfect or impulsive decision making.* Complex problem solving involves lots of working memory to keep multiple things in mind at once and then process them all together. For example, thinking about how a potential appointment fits into your schedule requires you to remember the rest of the day's commitments, think about what can get shuffled around versus what can't, factor in travel time, etc. People with ADHD are more likely to drop one or more important elements and thereby get themselves into trouble (e.g., forget about another meeting that will conflict with the new appointment). This looks like bad judgment, but their decision making process actually works fine; the real problem is that their weak memory causes them to not consider all the relevant information.

■ *Misplacing things.* You're more likely to remember where you put something if you make a mental note of it at the time. Unfortunately, many people with ADHD quickly drop that thought from their working memory because they move too quickly to the next task so that it never gets registered in their long-term memory. For example, if you put your keys down on the counter but immediately focus your attention on checking the answering machine, you probably won't have much of a memory of where the keys are, especially if this isn't where they normally go. The next day will then be a scramble as you run around the house trying to find your keys since there isn't much to pull out of your long-term memory.

■ *Forgetting what you are told.* If your working memory doesn't hold a necessary piece of information firmly enough, it gets knocked out by other information and lost before being transferred into long-term memory. This can make you look forgetful or even hard of hearing.

■ *Reading is uninteresting.* Reading requires a lot of working memory to keep your attention on the page and hold all those words in mind so that you can understand what the author is saying. People with ADHD find their attention going in and out, so it makes it difficult to understand what they are reading when they missed half the page that came before it. This makes reading frustrating, boring, and confusing, causing them to have to re-read in order to understand everything. As a result, they tend to avoid reading. (You can explain this to others by asking how much they would enjoy reading if random sentences and paragraphs were deleted, so they had to try to make sense out of what was left.)

■ *Experiential learners.* Many people with ADHD learn better by doing something than by reading or hearing about it. This is because actively engaging in a task requires less working memory than remembering what one was told, picturing oneself doing the task, and then applying it later. Unfortunately, few classrooms are set up this way (but some on-the-job training is).

Hang in There!

We've now identified some of the difficulties that can come from a weak working memory. It's important to identify the problems before getting into solutions. You may feel worse now because you're more aware of your struggles (and maybe even discovered some problems you didn't realize you had!). You may feel discouraged at this point if you feel like you have more problems than solutions. Hang in there! We'll get to the solutions next.

Identify Your Strategies

Let's now take a look at potential strategies to address these working memory struggles. This is where things begin to get better.

Some people have more struggles at work or school, while others have more challenges at home. Each of these parts of your life places different demands on you and also offers different supports, so you may perform really well in one but barely hold it together in the other. Because of this potential difference, you may find it helpful to practice new strategies more in one setting than in the other.

Or you may find that you have some of the same struggles in both situations. If this is the case, some of the same strategies may work in both places. This will provide some helpful carry-over benefit from practicing the same strategies throughout your day. You may also find that some strategies work better in one situation than in the other simply because the two situations are too different from each other. Do whatever works best.

The goal here is to go through the process of identifying targeted strategies based on your strengths, weaknesses, and what you need to get done. Some strategies will just be a better fit for you. Like many other situations in life, you're more likely to arrive at the best solutions if you follow a good process of evaluating your options. This will take some work, but it will be worth it. Also, because you're going to do it step by step, it should feel more manageable and less overwhelming and be more productive.

Working Memory Strategies Key Concepts

Most of the strategies that make the most of your working memory will fall under one of these basic ideas. By simplifying all those other strategies down to three basic ideas, it's easier to learn the concepts and apply them later.

■ Make important tasks and items stand out more to make it more likely that your attention will stay focused on them.

■ The fewer distractions, the easier it is to stay focused on and remember what you should.

■ Write things down rather than try to keep it all in your head.

Suggested Working Memory Strategies

Let's start things off with a list of strategies that tend to be helpful for working memory weaknesses so you can see where we're going. Some of these strategies may jump out at you—good!

Circle the **U** in the margin next to the strategies that you have used in the past and circle the **T** next to the ones that you haven't used before but think you might benefit from trying.

After each suggested strategy, write out:

1. If you've ever tried a particular strategy, how did it work for you? (past experiences)

2. What obstacles might get in the way of you using this strategy more often now? (obstacles)

3. How or where could you use this strategy more often? (use it more)

Key Concept: Make important tasks and items stand out more to make it more likely that your attention will stay focused on them.

U T *Do it right away.* Rather than hold a thought in working memory where it might get knocked out, do the task right away when it is still strongly held in your working memory (i.e., don't tell yourself, "I'll do that in a minute.").

Past experiences: _____

Obstacles: _____

Use it More: _____

U T *Use items as their own reminders.* If you need to do something with an item but can't do it right away, take it out and put it where you can see it so that it reminds you to do it. (This works only if you don't have a thousand other things out.)

Past experiences: _____

Obstacles: _____

Use it More: _____

U T *Take a reminder item with you.* If you get interrupted but want to come back to your original task, bring a reminder with you. For example, if you need to finish folding the laundry, bring a sock along with you when you answer the door.

Past experiences: _____

Obstacles: _____

Use it More: _____

U T *Ask for a reminder.* If you're in the middle of something ask a coworker to remind you later, for example after the meeting or to send you an email rather than asking you for something while passing in the hallway. (You need to be careful not to over-rely on others, but this is a valid technique when used appropriately—see Chapter 4: Work as a Team for more information.)

Past experiences: _____

Obstacles: _____

Use it More: _____

U T   *Highlight important information.* Brightly color important items or pieces of information so they stand out more from everything else. For example, tag certain emails as urgent or scribble a big red star on an envelope that you need to do something with.

Past experiences: _____

Obstacles: _____

Use it More: _____

U T   *Put up a note.* Tape up a reminder about something you are working on, such as a reminder to drink more water. You can also use visual reminders such as a picture of a well-organized closet to remind you to hang things back up or a hanging a bathing suit somewhere conspicuous to remind you about your diet.

Past experiences: _____

Obstacles: _____

Use it More: _____

Key Concept: The fewer distractions, the easier it is to stay focused on and remember what you should.

U T   *Reduce distractions.* The fewer stimuli and thoughts that are competing for your attention and working memory, the easier it is to stay focused on what you should. For example, turn off your cell phone, close your office door, ask not to be interrupted, use a whitenoise machine to block outside noises, etc.

Past experiences: _____

Obstacles: _____

Use it More: _____

U T   *Get rid of stuff.* The less stuff you have, the easier it is to organize and manage what's left. Usually the first step in getting organized is reducing the overall volume of stuff. Make some hard choices about what deserves to be kept and what doesn't—there's probably a lot more that you can live without than you will initially think.

Past experiences: _____

Obstacles: _____

Use it More: _____

U T *Bring less stuff in.* Related to the prior point, the less stuff that enters your life, house, or workplace, the less you have to deal with. Resist the temptation to acquire some new item by reminding yourself of the additional work later when you have to find a place for it and put it away.

Past experiences: _____

Obstacles: _____

Use it More: _____

U T *Put things away.* The less stuff you have out, the easier it is to keep your attention on what you're currently working on, especially after an interruption. On your computer, close unnecessary windows and programs.

Past experiences: _____

Obstacles: _____

Use it More: _____

U T *Remove yourself from mailing lists.* Whether it's email lists or listserves, unsubscribe from emails that you never really get around to reading. Don't ask for additional information to be sent to your house and don't renew magazines that you're not reading often enough. For emails, delete the junk right away. For mail, place a recycling bin near the door and quickly toss the junk.

Past experiences: _____

Obstacles: _____

Use it More: _____

U T *Limit the activities you get involved in.* Whether at work or in your personal life, make good choices about what you add to your plate. Consider to what extent an activity adds value to your life compared to the additional stress it will create, at least at this time.

Past experiences: _____

Obstacles: _____

Use it More: _____

U   T   *Cross off/delete items from your to-do list.* Once you complete a task, get it off your to-do list so it doesn't slow you down in finding the next important task. You should also delete those tasks that you have come to decide won't be completed because they no longer make the cut.

Past experiences: _____

Obstacles: _____

Use it More: _____

Key Concept: Write things down rather than try to keep it all in your head.

U   T   *Write yourself a reminder.* If you can't do something right away, capture the thought immediately on a to-do list, Post-It note, in your schedule, by leaving yourself a voicemail or email, or setting an alarm to remind you later.

Past experiences: _____

Obstacles: _____

Use it More: _____

U   T   *Snooze your alarms.* If you're not able to respond immediately to an alarm, don't turn it off completely and try to hold the task in your working memory. Instead, snooze the alarm so it goes off again. If you really don't have time to do the designated task now, then set the alarm again for another time.

Past experiences: _____

Obstacles: _____

Use it More: _____

U   T   *Write out complex problems.* Rather than try to keep everything in your mind, write out all the elements in a complex problem. Sometimes this is as simple as scribbling on the back of an envelope. For example, when planning how long something will take, write down each step and your time estimate, then add them all up. Or write out a shopping list of all the materials you will need for a project.

Past experiences: _____

Obstacles: _____

Use it More: _____

U T *Write out or use notes for multistep directions.* Use notes to keep you from skipping steps. Refer back to your notes and check off completed steps. Perhaps jot down additional notes or reminders for later as you move along.

Past experiences: _____

Obstacles: _____

Use it More: _____

Your Own Working Memory Strategies

There's a lot to be learned from past experiences. If it worked once, it might work again. Perhaps you kind of drifted away from a habit that was actually pretty good. Maybe you got bored with it. Maybe your habit got interrupted and you never came back to it. It happens. So maybe you just need to blow the dust off and use it again.

Think back on your past experiences over the years. What strategies have you used that have been helpful in making the most of your working memory? Even though no strategy works perfectly, there had to be some that you used that were helpful and increased your batting average. And if they were helpful, they were probably consistent with the strategies that make the most of people's working memory. Understanding how that works makes it more likely that you can apply them effectively to future challenges.

So let's identify those good strategies, understand how they are based in how your working memory functions, and then apply them forward. It might be helpful to think about how a particular strategy fits into the key concepts for working memory strategies, so I've included them below, as well. We'll answer the same questions that we did above.

Under each key concept, write out:

1. What strategy did you use?

2. How did this strategy work for you in the past?

3. What obstacles might get in the way of you using this strategy more often now?

4. How or where could you use this strategy more often?

Key Concept: Make important stimuli stand out more to make it more likely that your attention will stay focused on them.

Strategy: _____

Past Experiences: _____

Obstacles: _____

Use it More: _____

Strategy: _____

Past Experiences: _____

Obstacles: _____

Use it More: _____

Key Concept: The fewer distractions, the easier it is to stay focused on and remember what you should.

Strategy: _____

Past Experiences: _____

Obstacles: _____

Use it More: _____

Strategy: _____

Past Experiences: _____

Obstacles: _____

Use it More: _____

Key Concept: Write things down rather than try to keep it all in your head.

Strategy: _____

Past Experiences: _____

Obstacles: _____

Use it More: _____

Strategy: _____

Past Experiences: _____

Obstacles: _____

Use it More: _____

Apply Your Strategies

Choose Your Targeted Strategies

Look back at the suggested strategies and your own strategies from above. Choose one to three strategies to work on first—pick a manageable number so you can do it well. You may want to look back at the section on Fallout from Working Memory Weaknesses (page 40) and match your strategies to your struggles.

Although it's tempting to jump headfirst into the deep end and start with the places that you're struggling the most, it may be worth getting your feet wet on some smaller and more manageable struggles first. These easier successes will teach you some helpful lessons that you can use when tackling the thornier problems. There's also nothing like success as a motivator.

★ Write down which strategies you are planning to try first:

1. _____
2. _____
3. _____

It's better to focus on just a few changes first. Once you have these down, come back and add in some other strategies.

4. _____
5. _____
6. _____
7. _____
8. _____

Create Opportunities to Practice

Practice makes perfect. Or at least better. Although it's likely that your life will throw you plenty of opportunities to apply these new strategies, it can also be helpful to intentionally create or anticipate situations to practice these strategies.

Strategy: *Put up a note* _____

When and where can I apply this strategy? *Write big work deadlines in marker & tape up next to desk*

How do I know that this strategy is working? *By being more aware of deadlines, I plan my time better and have less to do at the end*

Strategy: _____

When and where can I apply this strategy? _____

How do I know that this strategy is working? _____

Strategy: _____

When and where can I apply this strategy? _____

_____

How do I know that this strategy is working? _____

_____

Strategy: _____

When and where can I apply this strategy? _____

_____

How do I know that this strategy is working? _____

_____

Make the Commitment

Once you have your targeted strategies identified, you need to make a commitment to apply them. A strategy is only as good as your commitment. Because this is a workbook, you only have yourself to answer to (which is ultimately all you have even when someone else is involved). I can guarantee that the strategies in this book, and probably most of the strategies you come up with, are good ones. They will get the job done. It all comes down to using them.

So I encourage you to take the pledge below. But don't do this lightly—think about it. Maybe take a day or a week to think about it. If you're going to do this, give it your best effort. You deserve it.

My Pledge

I want a better life, so I commit to:

■ Taking chances and trying something new.

■ Doing my best to use these strategies diligently, even when I don't feel like it.

■ Being open to learning from these experiences.

■ Being flexible when a strategy isn't working.

■ Only abandoning a strategy when I can replace it with another strategy that may work better.

_____   _____
Signature   Date

See the Rewards

We're more likely to start and maintain behaviors that are being rewarded, so let's talk about those all-important rewards. They come in a number of different shapes and sizes, so let's not miss any—the more rewards, the better.

Automatic Rewards

Some rewards are directly tied to our behavior. For example:

- *Inherent feelings of satisfaction/pride.* Even if no one else notices, we notice and feel good about having done something well.

- *Natural consequences.* These are rewards that come from the world around us, like when someone offers a compliment. Or getting a good seat at the movies by showing up early.

It may be helpful to make a point of looking for and noticing these rewards. The hectic pace of life makes it easy to miss them—which then makes it easier to drop off from those good habits, even when they're working. Since you're more likely to find what you're actively looking for, let's identify what these rewards would be.

If I used these strategies diligently, I would feel:

_____

_____

_____

_____

_____

_____

_____

_____

_____

If I used these strategies diligently, I would expect these natural consequences:

_____

_____

_____

_____

_____

_____

_____

_____

_____

_____

_____

Reward Yourself

Sometimes the inherent rewards and natural consequences aren't enough to push us over the edge to do something. This is when self-administered rewards come in handy. For example, "I will let myself do some actual woodworking after I clean up my shop." Or "I can check the sports scores after I finish these work emails."

Sometimes the reward is a good thing, whereas at other times the reward is just less bad than the first task. For example, "I will read this magazine article after I finish that technical report." Starting with the less desirable task creates an incentive to get to the more desirable task.

Think about some rewards that you can put in place for using your strategies. The reward needs to be good enough that it is actually motivating (but not so good that you'll skip the work and just take the reward).

If I use these strategies consistently, I will earn these rewards:

_____

_____

_____

_____

_____

_____

_____

_____

_____

Fine-tune Your Approach

Learn from Setbacks

You may find that it's much harder than you thought to apply your targeted strategies and make progress on the struggles that you first decided to focus on. This is normal and often expectable. Life is a constant process of trying things and learning from the feedback. If you get stuck, take a few moments to think about it and learn some valuable lessons.

Why was this harder than I expected?

_____

_____

_____

_____

_____

_____

_____

_____

_____

What obstacles are getting in my way?

_____

_____

_____

_____

_____

_____

_____

_____

_____

What lessons have I learned from this?

_____

_____

_____

_____

_____

_____

_____

_____

What would need to change in order to make it worth attempting this again?

_____

_____

_____

_____

_____

_____

_____

_____

_____

How can I apply these lessons to my next efforts?

_____

_____

_____

_____

_____

_____
_____
_____
_____
_____

Based on these lessons, what would be a good area to focus on next?

_____
_____
_____
_____
_____
_____
_____
_____
_____
_____
_____
_____

The Big Picture: Refine Your Approach

As we talked about in Chapter 3: Reality-Based Motivation, we learn from our experiences and apply those lessons forward. Life is a constant learning process. Now that you've been applying your targeted strategies for a few days or weeks, what lessons have you learned? If you take a few moments, I guarantee you will come up with some productive ideas, even if you've already done this a few times in other chapters. As you keep moving through the workbook, you will continue to figure out new things.

Lessons learned about my strategies:

_____
_____
_____
_____
_____
_____

_____

_____

_____

_____

Lessons learned about how my brain works:

_____

_____

_____

_____

_____

_____

_____

_____

_____

_____

_____

Lessons learned about how I motivate myself:

_____

_____

_____

_____

_____

_____

_____

_____

_____

_____

_____

Lessons learned about my workplace:

_____

_____

_____

_____

_____

_____

_____

_____

Lessons learned about my home life:

_____

_____

_____

_____

_____

_____

_____

_____

_____

Lessons learned about using this workbook:

_____

_____

_____

_____

_____

_____

_____

_____

_____

_____

CHAPTER 7

SENSE OF TIME: IT CAN'T BE 5:00 ALREADY!

What the Sense of Time Is

We all have an internal clock that tells us how much time has passed. For some people this clock ticks loudly and consistently, and they're pretty good at judging the passage of time. They use that knowledge to guide their behavior and to make necessary adjustments, such as speeding up when running low on time or re-prioritizing their activities to get the most important tasks completed when circumstances change. They have a loose schedule in mind, and they know where they are in relation to that schedule—what they have left to do and how much time they have to do it.

This sense of time is extremely important in today's society, not just at work but also with family and friends. Almost all parts of life require planning, forethought, and otherwise remembering what needs doing and, just as important, *when* it needs to be done. Some tasks, like meetings, have specific start times, and there is very little wiggle room. Other activities, like going to the bank, have a span of time during which the activity can occur (today from 9-5), which makes for a bigger target but you still need to get there within that range. Showing up at 8:00 is no more helpful than showing up at 6:00, and showing up five minutes after the bank closed doesn't do you any more good than not showing up at all. So it's all about doing the right things at the right times.

The sense of time comes out of our working memory. By remembering and tracking events in our working memory, we become aware of the passage of time. This then leads into prospective memory (remembering to do something at a future time), which will be covered in the next chapter. As I said before, the executive functions are all related and always work together, so it's difficult sometimes to talk about one in isolation.

Identify Your Struggles

Good solutions begin with a clear understanding of the problem. We'll begin here by listing the ways that sense of time weaknesses tend to affect someone's day to day life. You will then have some room to write other ways that your sense of time affects your life. Having this all in one place will make it easier to prioritize which areas to focus on first when we get to the strategies section.

Fallout from Sense of Time Weaknesses

People with ADHD usually know what they need to do but have trouble doing it at the best times. Their internal clock ticks too softly, so it doesn't guide their behavior reliably enough. As a result, they may stay absorbed in fun activities when they should transition to more obligatory, less fun activities. Or if they are doing something important and relevant, they may not notice what time it is and that they should have shifted to something else, like going to a meeting, getting to bed, or picking up the kids.

We can informally call this poor time management. That is, they don't manage their activities most effectively in relation to the time that they have available. They may create a great plan, but then get off track if they spend too long on some activities and not enough on others. The problem is that they don't stop occasionally to see what time it is and how much time they have left, assess their progress on their various activities, and adjust their plans if necessary in order to make best use of that time.

Weaknesses in the sense of time tend to create common and predictable struggles in daily life. For example:

■ *Time is very fluid.* Although time can fly when you're having fun, it can really crawl when you're doing something boring. More so than for most other people, time can be extremely fluid for people with ADHD. When doing something boring like vacuuming or paperwork, what feels like an hour may be as little as ten minutes (which is a horrible realization). So it takes more force of will to spend the necessary time on boring activities. On the other hand, when doing something fun an hour can feel like ten minutes, so they may spend more time than they planned or realize. This makes it very difficult to stick to a schedule if they don't accurately feel the passage of time.

■ *Underestimate time required.* Because time can be so fluid for them, many people with ADHD aren't good at predicting how long things will take. When planning ahead, they tend to underestimate more than they overestimate. They may use "best-case-scenario planning," basing predictions on how long it would take if everything fell into place perfectly without unexpected detours or delays. Of course, rarely does life cooperate so fully, so they tend to get crunched on time when something takes longer than they planned on. (Some of this is also based in difficulties with getting going on things until the pressure of the last minute drives them into action, which is covered further in Chapter 10: Self-Activation).

■ *Overestimate their ability to break away from an activity or limit how much time to give it.* Related to the previous bullet, they may overestimate their ability to dip into an activity for a brief period of time and then jump back out (e.g., "I'm just going to check the sports scores before I go."; "It will only take me two minutes to write that email."). They are especially prone to getting stuck on enjoyable activities and not realize that too much time is passing, especially if they encounter new, interesting elements (e.g., finding many other interesting recipes in a new cookbook) or unforeseen hurdles (e.g., one of the ingredients needs to be prepared separately). This reflects two different but related problems: 1. Being too optimistic about their ability to do one discreet task and then shift gears, 2. Losing track of the time once they are engaged in the task.

■ *Hyperfocus and miss transition points.* Hyperfocus is often described as really good attention, which is sort of accurate, but not entirely. More accurately, it's unbroken attention. People gets so absorbed in the current task that they lose track of the time that is passing—time doesn't enter their awareness. This is more likely to happen with enjoyable activities, where they can really get in the zone. Because time disappears, they don't transition to some new activity when they had planned to but don't realize it until it's too late. This is fundamentally different from the times when people make a conscious choice to continue in an activity, despite the consequences (although it can look the same to other people).

■ *Run late.* In order to get somewhere on time, we need to leave on time (barring unforeseen circumstances). Even with a good plan in mind, people with ADHD tend not to realize that they are approaching the time to leave. Their internal alarm clocks don't go off at the right time. As a result, they continue on with other activities rather than get ready to go. When they do suddenly realize what time it is, it's later than they had hoped. Underestimating the time required also contributes to running late.

- ◼ *Miss deadlines.* By not planning their time effectively and accurately, people with ADHD often don't give themselves enough time to do what they need to do. It can look like the task wasn't important to them, but it's actually more a problem of not starting it early enough. Once again, by the time they realize that they are going to run out of time, it's too late to change it.

- ◼ *Seen as a time waster.* Because they don't make best use of the time that they have available, they are often criticized for the choices they make, such as doing less important tasks first and then not getting to more important tasks. Although in reality there may not have been a conscious choice to skip the more important tasks it can look that way to others, which has negative social repercussions. In these cases, perception is reality until proven otherwise.

- ◼ *Get into bed too late.* In order to get into bed on time, a lot of the right things need to happen through the day. Because of their difficulties with managing their time, people with ADHD are often playing catch up, which ultimately pushes their bed time later. They also may not track the passage of time through the unstructured evening hours at home, so they aren't ready for bed or don't realize that it's bedtime. This is not a trivial matter. Sleeping in the next day can start that day off on the wrong foot. More insidious, sleep deprivation reduces our sense of time and makes for a less productive and enjoyable day, which leads to further troubles.

- ◼ *Speeding.* One way to make up for leaving too late is to drive faster. While this works to a point, it also puts the driver at risk for tickets and accidents. If you've been lucky so far, the research clearly shows that this habit will catch up with you in potentially very serious ways. (Not that I'm perfect.) Less dramatically, scrambling to get out the door can be stressful for yourself and others and lead to arguments and accusations.

- ◼ *Leave things behind.* Scrambling to get out the door robs you of a calm moment to stop and think about what you need to take with you, so things get left behind, which causes other problems.

Hang in There!

We've now identified some of the difficulties that can come from a weak sense of time. It's important to identify the problems before getting into solutions. You may feel worse now because you're more aware of your struggles (and maybe even discovered some problems you didn't realize you had!). You may feel discouraged at this point if you feel like you have more problems than solutions. Hang in there! We'll get to the solutions next.

Identify Your Strategies

Let's now take a look at potential strategies to address these sense of time struggles. This is where things begin to get better.

Some people have more struggles at work or school, while others have more challenges at home. Each of these parts of your life places different demands on you and also offers different supports, so you may perform really well in one but barely hold it together in the other. Because of this potential difference, you may find it helpful to practice new strategies more in one setting than in the other.

Or you may find that you have some of the same struggles in both situations. If this is the case, some of the same strategies may work in both places. This will provide some helpful carry-over benefit from practicing the same strategies throughout your day. You may also find that some strategies work better in one situation than in the other simply because the two situations are too different from each other. Do whatever works best.

The goal here is to go through the process of identifying targeted strategies based on your strengths, weaknesses, and what you need to get done. Some strategies will just be a better fit for you. Like many other situations in life, you're more likely to arrive at the best solutions if you follow a good process of evaluating your options. This will take some work, but it will be worth it. Also, because you're going to do it step by step, it should feel more manageable and less overwhelming and be more productive.

Sense of Time Strategies Key Concepts

Most of the strategies that make the most of your sense of time will fall under one of these basic ideas. By simplifying all those other strategies down to three basic ideas, it's easier to learn the concepts and apply them later.

■ Supplement your internal sense of time with plenty of clocks and external reminders.

■ Use alarms and other limits to notify you that a specific time has arrived.

■ Use a schedule to plan out your time.

Suggested Sense of Time Strategies

Let's start things off with a list of strategies that tend to be helpful for sense of time weaknesses so you can see where we're going. Some of these strategies may jump out at you—good!

Circle the **U** in the margin next to the strategies that you have used in the past and circle the **T** next to the ones that you haven't used before but think you might benefit from trying.

After each suggested strategy, write out:

1. If you've ever tried a particular strategy, how did it work for you? (past experiences)

2. What obstacles might get in the way of you using this strategy more often now? (obstacles)

3. How or where could you use this strategy more often? (use it more)

Key Concept: Supplement your internal sense of time with plenty of clocks and external reminders.

U T *Liberally sprinkle clocks throughout your world.* The more clocks you can see (without having to look for them), the more likely it is that you will be aware of the time. This is a rather passive solution that won't solve all your problems, but is easy and a good place to start.

Past experiences: _____

Obstacles: _____

Use it More: _____

U T *Make a habit of checking the time regularly.* Consciously and intentionally make a point of checking the time throughout your day. It's difficult to manage time effectively if you don't know what time it is. These regular check-ins will make it less likely that time will slip by unnoticed.

Past experiences: _____

Obstacles: _____

Use it More: _____

U T *Wear an actual watch.* I know, your phone has the time on it. But, related to the last strategy, you're more likely to look at the time if it's on your wrist than if you have to pull out your phone.

Past experiences: _____

Obstacles: _____

Use it More: _____

U T *Wear a watch with a regular beep or vibe.* Many digital watches can be set to give a small beep or vibe at regular intervals, such as every fifteen minutes. These regular reminders notify you that another block of time has passed. They may also break your hyperfocus if you've been stuck on something too long. You can buy watches that vibe from www.watchminder.com and www.vibralite.com, as well as a pager-size version for your pocket or belt clip at www.invisibleclock.com. You can also download a variety of apps for your smartphone.

Past experiences: _____

Obstacles: _____

Use it More: _____

U T *"What should I be doing now?"* If you find yourself slapping your forehead too often and asking yourself why you spent so long on something, work on the habit of asking yourself, "What should I be doing now? Is this the best use of my time?" If it isn't, take a moment to think about it and then switch gears to something that might be better.

Past experiences: _____

Obstacles: _____

Use it More: _____

U   T   *Put up signs to keep you on schedule in the morning.* Time how long it takes to do your various morning activities (e.g., shower, get dressed, make breakfast, etc.). Then count time backwards from the time you need to be walking out the door and therefore when you need to be finishing each activity (e.g., finish breakfast at 8:30, get dressed by 8:10, out of the bathroom by 8:00, etc.). Then put up signs in each room that tell you when you should be moving on to the next activity. That way, you can easily tell whether you're on track to get out the door on time. This breaks a large span of time (like an hour) into chunks that are easier to keep track of (like fifteen minutes). You may also find it helpful to set alarms or use countdown timers if you're still missing those transition times. You may also need to pad your times more if you're consistently running over.

Key Concept: Use alarms and other limits to notify you that a specific time has arrived.

U   T   *Set an alarm.* Even the simplest cell phone has an alarm function. Rather than relying on your own internal clock, you can let a piece of technology let you know that a particular time has arrived. (In this case, we're only talking about time frames of less than a day. We will talk about longer lengths of time in the next chapter on prospective memory. Many of the same principles apply.)

Past experiences: _____

Obstacles: _____

Use it More: _____

U   T   *Use countdown timers.* You can use the countdown timer and alarm on your digital watch or smartphone, or buy a number of cheap and easily programmed kitchen timers to alert you that a designated amount of time has passed and it's time to do something else (e.g., get ready to leave, change the laundry, etc.). Once you set the timer, you no longer need to mentally track the time because the timer is doing it for you. If you're working at the computer, you can use Outlook or other programs to alert you.

Past experiences: _____

Obstacles: _____

Use it More: _____

U   T   *Set a bedtime alarm.* Late starts in the morning often begin with late bedtimes the night before. If you tend to get caught up in various activities and miss your bedtime, set an alarm to go off when it's time to start getting ready. Then obey it under all circumstances unless your house is on fire.

Past experiences: _____

Obstacles: _____

Use it More: _____

U T *Use browser add-ons to limit your online time.* The Internet is an easy place to lose track of time because one link leads to another and another…You can use browser add-ons (such as Leechblock for Firefox and Stayfocsd [yes, that is the correct spelling] for Google Chrome) to limit how much time you spend on particular sites as well as overall online, and even create black-out times where you can't access certain sites. If you know it's too hard to break away in the heat of the moment, you can limit yourself by setting these up ahead of time.

Past experiences: _____

Obstacles: _____

Use it More: _____

U T *Avoid engrossing activities.* If you know that you lose track of time when doing certain activities, then it's probably not worth starting them if you don't have enough time or if it's too close to a time when you have to do something else. It's usually easier to not start something than to pull yourself away once you've started. If you do decide to start it, then at least set an alarm to let you know that it's time to stop.

Past experiences: _____

Obstacles: _____

Use it More: _____

U T *Set your TV to turn itself off.* Many televisions have a sleep timer that will automatically turn the TV off after a certain amount of time or at a specific time.

Past experiences: _____

Obstacles: _____

Use it More: _____

U T *Put your lights on a timer.* You can replace the regular wall switch with a relatively inexpensive programmable switch or use a plug-in module that goes into the outlet and into which light cords are plugged. In either case, you program it to turn off the lights at a specific time. A suddenly dark room is hard, but not impossible, to miss. This probably works better at home than at work, if there's a room that you tend to spend too long in at night.

Past experiences: _____

Obstacles: _____

Use it More: _____

U T *Peg your schedule to someone else's.* By going to bed, waking up, and/or leaving the house, etc. at the same time as someone else in the house, you can follow that person's lead on what time it is and where in the process you should be. At work, you can match your schedule to someone else's, for example when it's time to leave for a meeting. You need to use this strategy wisely, but it can work very well.

Past experiences: _____

Obstacles: _____

Use it More: _____

Key Concept: Use a schedule to plan out your time.

U T   *Write down a schedule for the day (then check it).* Whether you use a formal schedule or scribble something out on the back of an envelope, create a plan for the day. It's impossible to know if you're ahead of or behind schedule if you don't know what your schedule is. You don't need to schedule every moment, but may want to schedule specific events (e.g., leave for bank at 3:30, do laundry before lunch). Of course once you've created your schedule, you need to refer back to it so that it can guide your actions. You may also find it helpful to write out the day's schedule and tape it up so you can see it easily.

Past experiences: _____

Obstacles: _____

Use it More: _____

U T   *Adjust your schedule as circumstances change.* Rarely does a day follow a schedule perfectly, so you will need to keep it in your pocket or have it nearby so it's always handy to refer to when something new comes up. Don't commit to anything new until you've checked to see how it fits into your overall plan.

Past experiences: _____

Obstacles: _____

Use it More: _____

U T   *Build in time to get ready.* A common place where people get behind is not factoring in time to get ready to go from one activity to another or to leave the house/office. Depending on the activity, you may need to add in this time—e.g., to leave for a business meeting at 2:00 you need to start gathering your materials, print the directions, walk to the car, etc. at 1:45.

Past experiences: _____

Obstacles: _____

Use it More: _____

U T   *Follow someone else's schedule.* If you have a similar schedule as a family member, roommate, or coworker, you can follow that person's lead to keep yourself on track. If it's acceptable, you can even ask for assistance (e.g., "Give a yell if I'm still in bed at 7:30."; "Let me know when you're getting ready to leave."). It isn't anyone else's job to force you to do anything, merely to let you know what time it is.

Past experiences: _____

Obstacles: _____

Use it More: _____

U   T   *Time how long things actually take.* Although life is unpredictable and erratic at times, there are certain activities that tend to repeat pretty regularly. It may be helpful to time how long it takes you to do them a few times, write down those times, and then refer back to them when making plans.

Past experiences: _____

Obstacles: _____

Use it More: _____

U   T   *Add 50% (or more) to all your estimates.* If you have an activity that you haven't timed (see prior strategy), then you need to guess how long it might take to accomplish. Everything takes longer than we think it will, so pad your estimates. If the stars align and you get done faster, consider it a gift of time. And like all gifts, don't count on getting one every day.

Past experiences: _____

Obstacles: _____

Use it More: _____

Your Own Sense of Time Strategies

There's a lot to be learned from past experiences. If it worked once, it might work again. Perhaps you kind of drifted away from a habit that was actually pretty good. Maybe you got bored with it. Maybe your habit got interrupted and you never came back to it. It happens. So maybe you just need to blow the dust off and use it again.

Think back on your past experiences over the years. What strategies have you used that have been helpful in making the most of your sense of time? Even though no strategy works perfectly, there had to be some that you used that were helpful and increased your batting average. And if they were helpful, they were probably consistent with the strategies that make the most of people's sense of time. Understanding how that works makes it more likely that you can apply them effectively to future challenges.

So let's identify those good strategies, understand how they are based in how your sense of time functions, and then apply them forward. It might be helpful to think about how a particular strategy fits into the key concepts for sense of time strategies, so I've included them below, as well. We'll answer the same questions that we did above.

Under each key concept, write out:

1. What strategy did you use?

2. How did this strategy work for you in the past?

3. What obstacles might get in the way of you using this strategy more often now?

4. How or where could you use this strategy more often?

Key Concept: Supplement your internal sense of time with plenty of clocks and external reminders.

Strategy: _____

Past Experiences: _____

Obstacles: _____

Use it More: _____

Strategy: _____

Past Experiences: _____

Obstacles: _____

Use it More: _____

Key Concept: Use alarms and other limits to notify you that a specific time has arrived.

Strategy: _____

Past Experiences: _____

Obstacles: _____

Use it More: _____

Strategy: _____

Past Experiences: _____

Obstacles: _____

Use it More: _____

Key Concept: Use a schedule to plan out your time.

Strategy: _____

Past Experiences: _____

Obstacles: _____

Use it More: _____

Strategy: _____

Past Experiences: _____

Obstacles: _____

Use it More: _____

Apply Your Strategies

Choose Your Targeted Strategies

Look back at the suggested strategies and your own strategies from above. Choose one to three strategies to work on first—pick a manageable number so you can do it well. You may want to look back at the section on Fallout from Sense of Time Weaknesses (page 59) and match your strategies to your struggles.

Although it's tempting to jump headfirst into the deep end and start with the places that you're struggling the most, it may be worth getting your feet wet on some smaller and more manageable struggles first. These easier successes will teach you some helpful lessons that you can use when tackling the thornier problems. There's also nothing like success as a motivator.

★ Write down which strategies you are planning to try first:

1. _____
2. _____
3. _____

It's better to focus on just a few changes first. Once you have these down, come back and add in some other strategies.

4. _____
5. _____
6. _____
7. _____
8. _____

Create Opportunities to Practice

Practice makes perfect. Or at least better. Although it's likely that your life will throw you plenty of opportunities to apply these new strategies, it can also be helpful to intentionally create or anticipate situations to practice these strategies.

Strategy: *Set a bedtime alarm* _____

When and where can I apply this strategy? *Each night, starting tonight.* *Use my cell phone alarm because it will be in my pocket*

How do I know that this strategy is working? *When the alarm goes off, I know that it's time to go to bed and am more likely to stop what I'm doing*

Strategy: _____

When and where can I apply this strategy? _____

_____

How do I know that this strategy is working? _____

_____

Strategy: _____

When and where can I apply this strategy? _____

_____

How do I know that this strategy is working? _____

_____

Strategy: _____

When and where can I apply this strategy? _____

_____

How do I know that this strategy is working? _____

_____

Make the Commitment

Once you have your targeted strategies identified, you need to make a commitment to apply them. A strategy is only as good as your commitment. Because this is a workbook, you only have yourself to answer to (which is ultimately all you have even when someone else is involved). I can guarantee that the strategies in this book, and probably most of the strategies you come up with, are good ones. They will get the job done. It all comes down to using them.

So I encourage you to take the pledge below. But don't do this lightly—think about it. Maybe take a day or a week to think about it. If you're going to do this, give it your best effort. You deserve it.

My Pledge

I want a better life, so I commit to:

- Taking chances and trying something new.

- Doing my best to use these strategies diligently, even when I don't feel like it.

- Being open to learning from these experiences.

- Being flexible when a strategy isn't working.

- Only abandoning a strategy when I can replace it with another strategy that may work better.

_____

Signature   Date

See the Rewards

We're more likely to start and maintain behaviors that are being rewarded, so let's talk about those all-important rewards. They come in a number of different shapes and sizes, so let's not miss any—the more rewards, the better.

Automatic Rewards

Some rewards are directly tied to our behavior. For example:

- *Inherent feelings of satisfaction/pride.* Even if no one else notices, we notice and feel good about having done something well.

- *Natural consequences.* These are rewards that come from the world around us, like when someone offers a compliment or getting a good seat at the movies by showing up early.

It may be helpful to make a point of looking for and noticing these rewards. The hectic pace of life makes it easy to miss them—which then makes it easier to drop off from those good habits, even when they're working. Since you're more likely to find what you're actively looking for, let's identify what these rewards would be.

If I used these strategies diligently, I would feel:

_____

_____

_____

_____

_____

_____

_____

_____

_____

_____

If I used these strategies diligently, I would expect these natural consequences:

_____

_____

_____

_____

_____

_____

_____

_____

_____

_____

_____

Reward Yourself

Sometimes the inherent rewards and natural consequences aren't enough to push us over the edge to do something. This is when self-administered rewards come in handy. For example, "I will let myself do some actual woodworking after I clean up my shop." Or "I can check the sports scores after I finish these work emails."

Sometimes the reward is a good thing, whereas at other times the reward is just less bad than the first task. For example, "I will read this magazine article after I finish that technical report." Starting with the less desirable task creates an incentive to get to the more desirable task.

Think about some rewards that you can put in place for using your strategies. The reward needs to be good enough that it is actually motivating (but not so good that you'll skip the work and just take the reward).

If I use these strategies consistently, I will earn these rewards:

_____

_____

_____

_____

_____

_____

_____

_____

_____

_____

Fine-tune Your Approach

Learn from Setbacks

You may find that it's much harder than you thought to apply your targeted strategies and make progress on the struggles that you first decided to focus on. This is normal and often expectable. Life is a constant process of trying things and learning from the feedback. If you get stuck, take a few moments to think about it and learn some valuable lessons.

Why was this harder than I expected?

_____

_____

_____

_____

_____

_____

_____

_____

_____

What obstacles are getting in my way?

_____

_____

_____

_____

_____

_____

_____

_____

_____

_____

What lessons have I learned from this?

_____

_____

_____

_____

_____

_____

_____

_____

_____

What would need to change in order to make it worth attempting this again?

_____

_____

_____

_____

_____

_____

_____

_____

_____

_____

How can I apply these lessons to my next efforts?

_____

_____

_____

_____

_____

_____

_____

_____

_____

Based on these lessons, what would be a good area to focus on next?

_____

_____

_____

_____

_____

_____

_____

_____

_____

_____

The Big Picture: Refine Your Approach

As we talked about in Chapter 3: Reality-Based Motivation, we learn from our experiences and apply those lessons forward. Life is a constant learning process. Now that you've been applying your targeted strategies for a few days or weeks, what lessons have you learned? If you take a few moments, I guarantee you will come up with some productive ideas, even if you've already done this a few times in other chapters. As you keep moving through the workbook, you will continue to figure out new things.

SECTION II Make Your Life Better

Lessons learned about my strategies:

_____

_____

_____

_____

_____

_____

_____

_____

_____

Lessons learned about how my brain works:

_____

_____

_____

_____

_____

_____

_____

_____

_____

Lessons learned about how I motivate myself:

_____

_____

_____

_____

_____

_____
_____
_____
_____
_____

Lessons learned about my workplace:

_____
_____
_____
_____
_____
_____
_____
_____
_____
_____

Lessons learned about my home life:

_____
_____
_____
_____
_____
_____
_____
_____
_____

Make Your Life Better

Lessons learned about using this workbook:

_____

_____

_____

_____

_____

_____

_____

_____

_____

_____

CHAPTER 8

PROSPECTIVE MEMORY: REMEMBERING TO REMEMBER

What Prospective Memory Is

Prospective memory is the ability of remembering to remember. It's the capacity to remind ourselves to do the right thing at the right time. It's the process of carrying an idea from one moment in time into the future when it is the right time to act on it, for example, your boss asking you in the morning to call an important client this afternoon or getting an idea in the shower that you should take a CD to a friend's house tonight. It's a matter of holding that idea on deck until you have the opportunity to act on it.

As you might guess, prospective memory is an outgrowth of working memory and the sense of time— we hold the idea in working memory until our sense of time tells us it's time to act.

The key to success with prospective memory is all about getting the timing right. For example, if you have to make a phone call after lunch, it isn't that helpful to think about it before lunch because you can't do it then. It's also not helpful to think about it when you're driving home and it's now too late to call. So it's a matter of setting off that internal alarm during the period of time where you can actually act on the idea. Remembering before that window of time and remembering afterwards doesn't get you much (except frustrated).

Sometimes that window of time is really big, like with a task that has to be completed some time next week. Sometimes the window is really small, like when you get a call in the middle of something and tell the person that you will call him/her right back. Or you want to remember to take your jacket from the coat room at the restaurant—your window of time is the few seconds as you're walking from the table to the door. (Oh well, I didn't like that jacket anyway.)

To make this even more complicated, sometimes you need to remember the idea in a specific place— for example, remembering to check the kind of replacement battery you need for one of your kids' toys when you're at home and can actually look at the battery. Remembering this at work or in the car doesn't help. The technical term for this is the *point of performance*—the place and time where you can actually do something about it. Writing a reminder note at work (when you realize you should check the battery) might help in a general way, but it isn't enough to complete the task because the toy is at home. So the trick here is to trigger this idea when you're at home and can shift gears from what you're doing to go look at the toy.

We all have dozens of these sorts of tasks to keep track of every day. As we move from childhood into adolescence and then adulthood, we're increasingly expected to remember these things for ourselves and to be less dependent on others reminding us. This has become increasingly challenging as we have more and more to keep track of and more and more distractions pulling at our attention. And even though smartphones can be more of a problem than a solution, one of the reasons why they are so popular is that our brains can't handle all the information we're trying to store, so we use electronic brains to do some of that work for us. We use to-do lists and alarms to remind us and use the various data features to do things in the moment (like transfer money between bank accounts or fire off an email) so that we don't need to remember to do them later. This spares us from needing to keep one more thing in prospective memory.

Even though to-do lists, notes, reminders, etc. can be really helpful tools to relieve us of some of that prospective memory burden, there is a limit to how much you can write down. There comes a point where we need to keep certain things in our heads through the flow of the day or we'll spend all of our time writing down reminders and no time doing anything. People who are good at juggling multiple tasks and returning to their original task after an interruption have a strong prospective memory. This is an important skill when it comes to managing a busy, complicated life at both work and home.

Identify Your Struggles

Good solutions begin with a clear understanding of the problem. We'll begin here by listing the ways that prospective memory weaknesses tend to affect someone's day to day life. You will then have some room to write other ways that your prospective memory affects your life. Having this all in one place will make it easier to prioritize which areas to focus on first when we get to the strategies section.

Fallout from Prospective Memory Weaknesses

A strong prospective memory is important in managing all the moving details and interruptions of life these days. I somewhat facetiously say that a weak prospective memory is where good intentions come to die. People with ADHD have trouble holding a thought from the moment that they think of it until the moment when it's the time to act. They have trouble bridging that gap in time, of carrying that thought reliably into the future. They mean well and they truly intend to follow through with what they promise, but somehow get lost along the way. Sometimes they forget the thought completely, whereas at other times they remember it when it's too late. When they disappoint others, there can be social fall-out. When they disappoint themselves, it's another blow to their self-esteem.

This forgetfulness is fundamentally different from situations in which someone consciously decides that she won't do something. When the situation is due to a failure to remember, the task doesn't even enter consciousness for a decision to be made—and that's the key difference. On these occasions, the ADHD person may be as surprised and disappointed as everyone else that the task wasn't completed. Although it can be difficult to tease apart whether someone truly forgot to do an undesirable task or just tried to get out of it, people with ADHD will have many more examples of situations where they forgot to do something and paid a high price for it, for example, late fees on missed payments, getting locked out of classes because they missed the registration period, concert tickets getting sold out before they remembered to buy them, etc. These are situations where the person has nothing to gain by avoiding the task. People with ADHD pay a price for it.

Weaknesses in prospective memory tend to create common and predictable struggles in daily life. For example:

- ■ *Do what they should, but later than they should.* Much of modern life requires the right timing, even in our increasingly 24/7 world. Some tasks can be done late, although with a price. For example, calling the plumber in the afternoon, instead of first thing, means another day with a stopped-up sink.

- *Miss the window of opportunity.* Some tasks can't be completed late, for example, forgetting to pick up dessert on the way home before company arrives. Once the person arrives at home, there isn't enough time to go back out to get the dessert. By the time it's remembered, it's too late.

- *Completely forget to do something.* Some tasks completely fall off the person's radar screen and are forgotten until some external reminder (like somebody asking about it) triggers the memory. Without that reminder, the memory would be completely gone—and sometimes even the reminder isn't enough to bring back any traces of the original event. (No, you never asked me to do that.)

- *Self-mistrust.* As much as we all like to think that we can count on ourselves to do what we say we will, the many examples of forgetfulness can justifiably erode the self-confidence of many adults with ADHD. They mean well, but learn to distrust their ability to reliably do what they need to do. When confronted with yet another situation where they dropped the ball, they may react by getting down on themselves or by becoming defensively angry. Both of these reactions are understandable, but they only make things worse.

- *Seen as unreliable.* Once the person with ADHD has established a track record of not doing enough of what he said he would, it's easy for others to stop asking. If the person with ADHD is lucky, the other person will see these lapses as unintentional and recognize that the person with ADHD does indeed mean well, but he may still not be included in certain activities.

- *Seen as irresponsible.* It's one thing to be seen as unreliable; it's another for that lack of reliability to be seen as intentional. Most people use their own experience to understand why other people do what they do, so someone who has a pretty decent memory will assume that the ADHD person purposely chose not to do something, since that would be the reason that the non-ADHD person didn't do something. Of course in this case, that conclusion assumes that the person with ADHD remembered the task, which he probably didn't. This isn't a problem of bad choices, it's a problem of bad remembering.

- *Cover-ups.* After dropping the ball too many times, it's tempting to lie about a task that they forgot to do, the idea being that they will then go ahead and do it and no one will be the wiser (assuming they actually remember to do it later, which sometimes they don't). This way the task gets done, and there is less drama. This is especially tempting when the other person's reactions are especially strong or critical. Where things break down is when the cover-up is somehow discovered, which creates even more drama.

- *Feel like they're always playing catch-up.* Because tasks are too easily forgotten they get pushed from one hour to the next and one day to the next, so there's a feeling of always being behind the eight ball on too many obligations.

- *Excessive late fees, lower credit scores, and higher interest rates.* Forgetting to pay their bills (or even to put it in the mail box once it is in the envelope) can quickly rack up late fees. Over time, this kills their credit score, even if they had more than enough money to pay the bill when it was due. This then leads to higher interest rates when borrowing money and perhaps larger deposits being required for certain transactions.

- *Expedited shipping costs, generally higher prices, and fewer options.* Many transactions benefit the early bird. People who don't get a quick jump on things often wind up having to pay more. For example, overnight shipping will make up for the fact that something was ordered late, but comes at a high price. Other items, like airline tickets or Halloween costumes, become more expensive and/or offer fewer options as time goes by.

- *Never ending and constantly expanding to-do lists.* Although to-do lists can be a great tool, it can be depressing to feel like they never put enough of a dent in their obligations or that new tasks show up quicker than their ability to knock off the old ones. In addition, important tasks may get lost in a long list of less important items if the person forgets about them.

Hang in There!

We've now identified some of the difficulties that can come from a weak prospective memory. It's important to identify the problems before getting into solutions. You may feel worse now because you're more aware of your struggles (and maybe even discovered some problems you didn't realize you had!). You may feel discouraged at this point if you feel like you have more problems than solutions. Hang in there! We'll get to the solutions next.

Identify Your Strategies

Let's now take a look at potential strategies to address these prospective memory struggles. This is where things begin to get better.

Some people have more struggles at work or school, while others have more challenges at home. Each of these parts of your life places different demands on you and also offers different supports, so you may perform really well in one but barely hold it together in the other. Because of this potential difference, you may find it helpful to practice new strategies more in one setting than in the other.

Or you may find that you have some of the same struggles in both situations. If this is the case, some of the same strategies may work in both places. This will provide some helpful carry-over benefit from practicing the same strategies throughout your day. You may also find that some strategies work better in one situation than in the other simply because the two situations are too different from each other. Do whatever works best.

The goal here is to go through the process of identifying targeted strategies based on your strengths, weaknesses, and what you need to get done. Some strategies will just be a better fit for you. Like many other situations in life, you're more likely to arrive at the best solutions if you follow a good process of evaluating your options. This will take some work, but it will be worth it. Also, because you're going to do it step by step, it should feel more manageable and less overwhelming and be more productive.

Prospective Memory Strategies Key Concepts

Most of the strategies that make the most of your prospective memory will fall under one of these basic ideas. By simplifying all those other strategies down to two basic ideas, it's easier to learn the concepts and apply them later.

■ Support your working memory by using external reminders to keep the task in your awareness.

■ Support your sense of time by setting up reminders and alarms that will trigger your memory at the right time and place.

Suggested Prospective Memory Strategies

Let's start things off with a list of strategies that tend to be helpful for prospective memory weaknesses so you can see where we're going. Some of these strategies may jump out at you—good!

Circle the **U** in the margin next to the strategies that you have used in the past and circle the **T** next to the ones that you haven't used before but think you might benefit from trying.

After each suggested strategy, write out:

1. If you've ever tried a particular strategy, how did it work for you? (past experiences)

2. What obstacles might get in the way of you using this strategy more often now? (obstacles)

3. How or where could you use this strategy more often? (use it more)

Key Concept: Support your working memory by using external reminders to keep the task in your awareness.

U T *Do it now.* Don't rely on your prospective memory more than you have to. Given that life is hectic and sometimes unpredictable, it's often a setup for trouble to rely on our prospective memory. Good intentions often aren't enough; it's often best just to do the task immediately. When you start telling yourself, "I'll do that in a minute," remind yourself of what might happen if you then get side-tracked and forget it. Think vividly of the later stress, the potential social cost, the additional financial price, etc. If you really can't do the task immediately, then create a reminder for later.

Past experiences: _____

Obstacles: _____

Use it More: _____

U T *Use a to-do list.* Whether you use a paper or electronic version, use a to-do list to capture all those various tasks as soon as you think of them. Cross off completed tasks, as well as those tasks that you've decided you won't get to, so that you don't lose important items in a long list of minor matters.

Past experiences: _____

Obstacles: _____

Use it More: _____

U T *Use items as their own reminders.* Place an item where it will serve as its own reminder. For example, if you realize tonight that you need to take an umbrella tomorrow, then place it in front of the door so you can't leave the house without tripping over it.

Past experiences: _____

Obstacles: _____

Use it More: _____

U T *Place items in your path or in your line of sight.* Put necessary items where you will see them without having to remember to look for them. For example, when going out to eat, put your bag on the floor on the side towards the door, not towards the wall. Think "out of sight, out of mind".

Past experiences: _____

Obstacles: _____

Use it More: _____

U T *Reduce clutter.* Items will serve as their own reminders more reliably if they don't get visually swallowed up by too much other stuff. The less you have competing for your visual attention, the more likely it is that you will spot your reminders.

Past experiences: _____

Obstacles: _____

Use it More: _____

Prospective Memory: Remembering to Remember

U T *Set up automatic debits/bill-pay and online banking.* By setting things up ahead of time, you don't need to remember to handle them later. You can reduce the number of late payments by setting up automatic debits that pull the money from your bank account or credit card. This may work better for the smaller bills, rather than a rent or mortgage payment that may risk an over-draft. (Over-draft protection is also a good idea.) For any remaining bills, online bill-pay gets the bills paid with a few clicks, which means you don't have to find a stamp and then remember to get the envelopes all the way to the mailbox (sitting on your desk doesn't count).

Past experiences: _____

Obstacles: _____

Use it More: _____

U T *Move forward (and don't waste time beating yourself up).* When you realize that something slipped through the cracks, jump in to fix it. You may not have the situation that you wish you did, so focus on determining what your current options are and what you can do about it now.

Past experiences: _____

Obstacles: _____

Use it More: _____

U T *Start an email but finish it later.* One strategy I personally use a lot is to start a new email by typing in the recipient and the subject line. When an email comes in that I definitely want to read later, I will click reply to make it an open email. By creating these open emails, I don't need to remember them because they're in my list of open windows. Whenever I click on my email program, I see all the emails I need to read/send, and that's my email to-do list. The idea is captured and I don't need to think about it because I regularly look through that list of open emails. This works really well when I don't have time to do all my emails but get an idea to email someone or want to take a quick look through what's come in.

Past experiences: _____

Obstacles: _____

Use it More: _____

U T *Open a new web page in your browser but don't actually look at it.* This is the same concept as the last strategy related to emails, but with web pages that I want to check out. The trick is to resist the temptation to "just take a quick look." Open the page and then immediately jump back to what you had been doing.

Past experiences: _____

Obstacles: _____

Use it More: _____

Key Concept: Support your sense of time by setting up reminders and alarms that will trigger your memory at the right time and place.

U T *Set an alarm.* Countdown timers and alarms are really good at keeping track of time so you don't need to do so. You can use electronic versions on your computer or smartphone or use cheap kitchen timers. Whatever you use, it needs to be easy to set quickly so you're more likely to use it.

Past experiences: _____

Obstacles: _____

Use it More: _____

U T *Obey the alarm or snooze it.* Once an alarm goes off, you need to do what the alarm is telling you to do. If you really aren't able to do it immediately, then snooze the alarm (rather than turn it off completely while telling yourself that you'll get to that in a minute) so you get another shot at it. The rule is "do it or snooze it".

Past experiences: _____

Obstacles: _____

Use it More: _____

U T *Leave notes where you need them.* Some tasks need to be remembered at specific locations, such as at home or work, while you're walking out the door, etc. Tape up or place a note in those places where you can act on the task.

Past experiences: _____

Obstacles: _____

Use it More: _____

U T *Leave yourself voicemails or emails.* You can call your home voicemail from work to remind yourself to do something there, and vice versa. Or send an email to your work account while at home or from your phone while out doing errands. This way you see the reminder at the place where you need it.

Past experiences: _____

Obstacles: _____

Use it More: _____

Prospective Memory: Remembering to Remember

U T *Scribble yourself a reminder and put it in your pocket.* This may be a middle step, where the note reminds you to put the task on your to-do list, take out the necessary item, etc., but it carries the idea from the moment of writing the note to a time where you can create a better reminder. If you keep your to-do list on your smartphone, then it will probably always be with you and easy to add items.

Past experiences: _____

Obstacles: _____

Use it More: _____

U T *Tie a string around your finger (metaphorically).* If you aren't able to access the necessary item or write yourself a note, use some other out of place item as a reminder. The key is that it has to be weird, random, or out of place enough that when you see it, it will catch your attention and remind you of what it represents. The item doesn't need to have any actual relationship to the task; for example, you can turn a chair upside-down to remind you to go to the bank.

Past experiences: _____

Obstacles: _____

Use it More: _____

U T *Ask for reminders.* It's often better to ask for some help rather than struggle on your own. You need to make sure that overall the relationship remains balanced, but this can be a great strategy, especially when the other person has a vested interest in something being completed on time. The agreement is that the reminder will be offered respectfully and accepted graciously. Everybody wins (which is much better than rolling the dice and hoping for the best).

Past experiences: _____

Obstacles: _____

Use it More: _____

U T *Use a paper schedule.* It's easier to do the right things at the right times if you have a plan about when those times should be. A written schedule also makes it less likely that you will double-book yourself when a task drops out of mind. Schedules work best when you make a point of not committing to anything without first checking your schedule and then putting the new task immediately into your schedule. Because paper schedules don't beep at you, you have to remember to check them. They work best for people who have lots of things to keep track of and are therefore frequently looking at their schedule. Every time they open the book, it provides a passive reminder about what's coming.

Past experiences: _____

Obstacles: _____

Use it More: _____

U T *Use an electronic schedule.* People who have fewer items on their schedule do better with an electronic version (including even the simple calendar on basic cell phones) that beeps at them when an important time has arrived. Because they don't access their schedules as frequently, they get fewer passive reminders and therefore need more active reminders.

Past experiences: _____

Obstacles: _____

Use it More: _____

U T *Enter tasks into your schedule.* You can use your schedule for more than just appointments and meetings. Some tasks don't need to be done at a specific time (such as running to the store or researching summer camps) but can easily be squeezed out of the day if you don't plan some specific time for them. Put these items into your schedule, too.

Past experiences: _____

Obstacles: _____

Use it More: _____

U T *Make your intentions clear.* If you do happen to forget something, make a point of acknowledging the effect that it had on the other person and then what you will do to remedy it. You will probably have a better impact if you talk specifically about how and when you will take care of the task and then show the person that you are writing a note or taking some other action, rather than simply trying to remember it.

Past experiences: _____

Obstacles: _____

Use it More: _____

Your Own Prospective Memory Strategies

There's a lot to be learned from past experiences. If it worked once, it might work again. Perhaps you kind of drifted away from a habit that was actually pretty good. Maybe you got bored with it. Maybe your habit got interrupted and you never came back to it. It happens. So maybe you just need to blow the dust off and use it again.

Think back on your past experiences over the years. What strategies have you used that have been helpful in making the most of your prospective memory? Even though no strategy works perfectly, there had to be some that you used that were helpful and increased your batting average. And if they were helpful, they were probably consistent with the strategies that make the most of people's prospective memory. Understanding how that works makes it more likely that you can apply them effectively to future challenges.

So let's identify those good strategies, understand how they are based in how your prospective memory functions, and then apply them forward. It might be helpful to think about how a particular strategy fits into the key concepts for prospective memory strategies, so I've included them below, as well. We'll answer the same questions that we did above.

Prospective Memory: Remembering to Remember

1. What strategy did you use?

2. How did this strategy work for you in the past?

3. What obstacles might get in the way of you using this strategy more often now?

4. How or where could you use this strategy more often?

Key Concept: Support your working memory by using external reminders to keep the task in your awareness.

Strategy: _____

Past Experiences: _____

Obstacles: _____

Use it More: _____

Strategy: _____

Past Experiences: _____

Obstacles: _____

Use it More: _____

Key Concept: Support your sense of time by setting up reminders and alarms that will trigger your memory at the right time and place.

Strategy: _____

Past Experiences: _____

Obstacles: _____

Use it More: _____

Strategy: _____

Past Experiences: _____

Obstacles: _____

Use it More: _____

Apply Your Strategies

Choose Your Targeted Strategies

Look back at the suggested strategies and your own strategies from above. Choose one to three strategies to work on first—pick a manageable number so you can do it well. You may want to look back at the section on Fallout from Prospective Memory Weaknesses (page 80) and match your strategies to your struggles.

Although it's tempting to jump headfirst into the deep end and start with the places that you're struggling the most, it may be worth getting your feet wet on some smaller and more manageable struggles first. These easier successes will teach you some helpful lessons that you can use when tackling the thornier problems. There's also nothing like success as a motivator.

★ Write down which strategies you are planning to try first:

1. _____
2. _____
3. _____

It's better to focus on just a few changes first. Once you have these down, come back and add in some other strategies.

4. _____
5. _____
6. _____
7. _____
8. _____

Create Opportunities to Practice

Practice makes perfect. Or at least better. Although it's likely that your life will throw you plenty of opportunities to apply these new strategies, it can also be helpful to intentionally create or anticipate situations to practice these strategies.

Strategy: *Leave yourself voicemails or emails*

When and where can I apply this strategy? *Leave messages on my work voicemail from home or cell when I remember I have to do something during business hours*

How do I know that this strategy is working? *I remember more of the things that I need to do and do them at the right times*

Strategy: _____

When and where can I apply this strategy? _____

_____

How do I know that this strategy is working? _____

_____

Strategy: _____

When and where can I apply this strategy? _____

_____

How do I know that this strategy is working? _____

_____

Strategy: _____

When and where can I apply this strategy? _____

_____

How do I know that this strategy is working? _____

_____

Make the Commitment

Once you have your targeted strategies identified, you need to make a commitment to apply them. A strategy is only as good as your commitment. Because this is a workbook, you only have yourself to answer to (which is ultimately all you have even when someone else is involved). I can guarantee that the strategies in this book, and probably most of the strategies you come up with, are good ones. They will get the job done. It all comes down to using them.

So I encourage you to take the pledge below. But don't do this lightly—think about it. Maybe take a day or a week to think about it. If you're going to do this, give it your best effort. You deserve it.

My Pledge

I want a better life, so I commit to:

- Taking chances and trying something new.

- Doing my best to use these strategies diligently, even when I don't feel like it.

- Being open to learning from these experiences.

- Being flexible when a strategy isn't working.

- Only abandoning a strategy when I can replace it with another strategy that may work better.

_____

Signature   Date

See the Rewards

We're more likely to start and maintain behaviors that are being rewarded, so let's talk about those all-important rewards. They come in a number of different shapes and sizes, so let's not miss any—the more rewards, the better.

Automatic Rewards

Some rewards are directly tied to our behavior. For example:

- *Inherent feelings of satisfaction/pride*. Even if no one else notices, we notice and feel good about having done something well.

- *Natural consequences*. These are rewards that come from the world around us, like when someone offers a compliment. Or getting a good seat at the movies by showing up early.

It may be helpful to make a point of looking for and noticing these rewards. The hectic pace of life makes it easy to miss them—which then makes it easier to drop off from those good habits, even when they're working. Since you're more likely to find what you're actively looking for, let's identify what these rewards would be.

If I used these strategies diligently, I would feel:

_____

_____

_____

_____

_____

_____

_____
_____
_____
_____

If I used these strategies diligently, I would expect these natural consequences:

_____
_____
_____
_____
_____
_____
_____
_____
_____
_____

Reward Yourself

Sometimes the inherent rewards and natural consequences aren't enough to push us over the edge to do something. This is when self-administered rewards come in handy. For example, "I will let myself do some actual woodworking after I clean up my shop." or "I can check the sports scores after I finish these work emails."

Sometimes the reward is a good thing, whereas at other times the reward is just less bad than the first task. For example, "I will read this magazine article after I finish that technical report." Starting with the less desirable task creates an incentive to get to the more desirable task.

Think about some rewards that you can put in place for using your strategies. The reward needs to be good enough that it is actually motivating (but not so good that you'll skip the work and just take the reward).

If I use these strategies consistently, I will earn these rewards:

_____
_____
_____
_____
_____

_____

_____

_____

_____

_____

Fine-tune Your Approach

Learn from Setbacks

You may find that it's much harder than you thought to apply your targeted strategies and make progress on the struggles that you first decided to focus on. This is normal and often expectable. Life is a constant process of trying things and learning from the feedback. If you get stuck, take a few moments to think about it and learn some valuable lessons.

Why was this harder than I expected?

_____

_____

_____

_____

_____

_____

_____

_____

_____

What obstacles are getting in my way?

_____

_____

_____

_____

_____

_____

_____

_____

_____

_____

What lessons have I learned from this?

_____

_____

_____

_____

_____

_____

_____

_____

_____

What would need to change in order to make it worth attempting this again?

_____

_____

_____

_____

_____

_____

_____

_____

_____

_____

How can I apply these lessons to my next efforts?

_____

_____

_____

_____

_____

_____

_____

_____

_____

_____

Based on these lessons, what would be a good area to focus on next?

_____

_____

_____

_____

_____

_____

_____

_____

_____

_____

The Big Picture: Refine Your Approach

As we talked about in Chapter 3: Reality-Based Motivation, we learn from our experiences and apply those lessons forward. Life is a constant learning process. Now that you've been applying your targeted strategies for a few days or weeks, what lessons have you learned? If you take a few moments, I guarantee you will come up with some productive ideas, even if you've already done this a few times in other chapters. As you keep moving through the workbook, you will continue to figure out new things.

Lessons learned about my strategies:

_____

_____

_____

_____

_____

_____

_____

_____

_____

_____

Lessons learned about how my brain works:

_____

_____

_____

_____

_____

_____

_____

_____

_____

Lessons learned about how I motivate myself:

_____

_____

_____

_____

_____

_____

_____

_____

_____

_____

Lessons learned about my workplace:

_____

_____

_____

_____

_____

_____

_____

_____

_____

_____

Lessons learned about my home life:

_____

_____

_____

_____

_____

_____

_____

_____

_____

_____

Lessons learned about using this workbook:

_____

_____

_____

_____

_____

_____

_____

_____

_____

CHAPTER 9

EMOTIONAL SELF-CONTROL: HAVING FEELINGS WITHOUT ACTING ON THEM

What Emotional Control Is

We use our emotions to inform our decisions and to guide our behavior. Our feelings can tell us a lot about a situation. They can also influence how we behave and make life richer and more interesting.

Children tend to have much stronger emotions than adults. When they get completely consumed by how they feel, kids don't just have feelings, they are their feelings. If they're angry, they see red and only red. If they're happy, everything is right with the world. Part of the job of parenting is to provide a buffer between kids and their feelings—"No, you can't hit your sister even if she knocked down your blocks."; "I know this playground is really fun, but we still need to get ready for dinner."

As kids become adults, they learn to temper their emotions. They can feel something but not lose themselves in that feeling or have it completely overwhelm their rational thinking (most of the time). Adults are still influenced by their feelings, but they have some greater perspective on it. For example, if they're angry they can control it rather than lashing out. If they feel disappointed they recognize that this will pass in time. If they're excited about going on vacation tomorrow they can still get things done today.

Perhaps because they don't feel their emotions as strongly, most adults are better able to display a watered-down version of their feelings. They may feel something strongly, but they don't wear their emotions on their sleeve as much. Adults are better able to consider the larger situation before expressing their feelings. They still have them but aren't as driven by them.

The ability to create this pause between emotion and action is important because it gives us objectivity when we can see beyond our initial reaction. This allows us to change how much the feeling colors our thoughts and drives our actions. For example, we may get angry at our boss but remember that it's kind of nice to continue getting a steady paycheck, so we don't tell him how we really feel, even when he deserves it. Adults are expected to be able to pause long enough to talk themselves down from their initial feeling and talk themselves out of acting rashly.

In addition, being able to view our feelings with objectivity gives us the ability to see someone else's perspective even when it differs from our own. We're able to set our feelings aside and see that someone else may feel differently about the same situation. For example, we may remember that our coworker is under a lot of pressure and therefore not take it personally when she comes across as demanding.

Finally, being able to exert at least some control over our feelings leads to motivation to start and stick with tasks and get things done. By focusing on the rewards for a job well done or some enjoyable aspect of the task, we create the appropriate feelings within ourselves when the task otherwise doesn't motivate us. We can self-generate motivation by bringing up the positive feelings that will come from completing this task or by wanting to avoid the negative feelings associated with missing a deadline. This is discussed further in the next chapter, Self-Activation.

Identify Your Struggles

Good solutions begin with a clear understanding of the problem. We'll begin here by listing the ways that emotional self-control weaknesses tend to affect someone's day to day life. You will then have some room to write other ways that your emotional self-control affects your life. Having this all in one place will make it easier to prioritize which areas to focus on first when we get to the strategies section.

Fallout from Emotional Self-Control Weaknesses

People with ADHD tend to feel and display their emotions more intensely compared to people without ADHD. Although it isn't part of the official diagnostic system (yet), people with ADHD are often known for their strong reactions. And not just anger—every feeling may be more intense. When it's the positive emotions such as happiness or humor, this can make people with ADHD more interesting and engaging. Unfortunately, anger and frustration tend to have the opposite effect.

In Chapter 5: Response Inhibition we talked about how people with ADHD have difficulty inhibiting responses (i.e., creating a pause between stimulus and response). Because of this, the executive functions have less space to operate in and the person tends to be too pulled by circumstances. One of the ways that this plays out is in the emotional reactions—the emotions get fired off, and the inhibitory part of their brains doesn't hold back that reaction enough. So out come the emotions at full force. Not only do people with ADHD tend to feel their emotions more strongly, they also tend to display their emotions more.

Weaknesses in emotional control tend to create common and predictable struggles in daily life. For example:

- *Show emotions more strongly.* Many adults with ADHD will have a poor poker face when they feel something strongly. They will show more of what they feel, compared to other adults who may feel it inside but not show so much outside. Although there are also times when this is neither good nor bad, there are times when the person is better served by not revealing so much (e.g., at a work meeting, with a frustrating child).

- *Behave spontaneously when strongly influenced by emotions.* People with ADHD are more likely to be guided by their strong feelings, whereas others may stop and think for a moment before acting. (By the way, it's labeled "spontaneous" if it works out well and "impulsive" or "irresponsible" if it doesn't.) Spontaneity can be fun as long as no one gets into trouble.

- *Lose the big picture.* Adults with ADHD are more prone to letting their initial feelings guide their behavior without considering this bigger context. Because they feel their emotions more strongly, they become absorbed in those feelings and have trouble seeing beyond the immediate situation. This makes for decisions that they may later regret (e.g., get excited about something at the store and buy it before considering how it fits in the budget).

- *Lose the other person's perspective.* Adults with ADHD are more prone to losing sight of someone else's perspective in the heat of the moment (although everyone loses that to some degree when fired up). They may see it more clearly afterward when things have cooled off, but it may be too late by then. This is one of the reasons that adults with ADHD are sometimes perceived as self-centered. It isn't really that they think only of themselves, it's just that they sometimes have a hard time seeing beyond their feelings in the moment to be able to appreciate another person's needs. (They sometimes also have trouble seeing beyond their emotions to see their own long-term needs). Unfortunately, apologies afterward aren't always enough to mend fences.

- *Impulsively say something they later regret.* When they get caught up in the feelings of the moment they may say something that they otherwise wouldn't. Often what they say is accurate and valid but comes across too strongly. Sometimes the person reacts to only part of the situation but would have responded differently if they had considered other aspects, in which case the response doesn't seem as fitting.

- *"Motivation deficit disorder."* People with ADHD have a harder time motivating themselves to start and finish tasks that aren't inherently interesting. This will be covered more fully in the next chapter on self-activation, but it begins with this difficulty with emotional control.

- *Strong displays of anger and frustration damage relationships.* It takes only a couple over the top outbursts (as defined by the other person) to undermine a lot of good interactions with family, friends, coworkers, and bosses.

- *Strong emotional reactions can go as quickly as they come.* Generally our emotions tend to come and go over relatively short periods of time. More intense emotions may last longer than milder emotions. As a result, other people may expect that the person with ADHD's strong feelings will last longer than they do, so they will be surprised when the person with ADHD has moved on so quickly.

- *Impulsively quit jobs.* Research has found that adults with ADHD are significantly more likely to impulsively quit a job. This has obvious implications for both their current finances as well as their ability to build seniority and also find a new job.

Hang in There!

We've now identified some of the difficulties that can come from a weak emotional self-control. It's important to identify the problems before getting into solutions. You may feel worse now because you're more aware of your struggles (and maybe even discovered some problems you didn't realize you had!). You may feel discouraged at this point if you feel like you have more problems than solutions. Hang in there! We'll get to the solutions next.

Identify Your Strategies

Let's now take a look at potential strategies to address these emotional self-control struggles. This is where things begin to get better.

Some people have more struggles at work or school, while others have more challenges at home. Each of these parts of your life places different demands on you and also offers different supports, so you may perform really well in one but barely hold it together in the other. Because of this potential difference, you may find it helpful to practice new strategies more in one setting than in the other.

Or you may find that you have some of the same struggles in both situations. If this is the case, some of the same strategies may work in both places. This will provide some helpful carry-over benefit from practicing the same strategies throughout your day. You may also find that some strategies work better in one situation than in the other simply because the two situations are too different from each other. Do whatever works best.

The goal here is to go through the process of identifying targeted strategies based on your strengths, weaknesses, and what you need to get done. Some strategies will just be a better fit for you. Like many other situations in life, you're more likely to arrive at the best solutions if you follow a good process of evaluating your options. This will take some work, but it will be worth it. Also, because you're going to do it step by step, it should feel more manageable and less overwhelming and be more productive.

Emotional Self-Control Strategies Key Concepts

Most of the strategies that make the most of your emotional self-control will fall under one of these basic ideas. By simplifying all those other strategies down to three basic ideas, it's easier to learn the concepts and apply them later.

- Manage your stress.

- The less strongly you feel an emotion, the easier it is to control it.

- Own up to your reactions.

Suggested Emotional Self-Control Strategies

Let's start things off with a list of strategies that tend to be helpful for emotional self-control weaknesses so you can see where we're going. Some of these strategies may jump out at you—good!

Circle the **U** in the margin next to the strategies that you have used in the past and circle the **T** next to the ones that you haven't used before but think you might benefit from trying.

After each suggested strategy, write out:

1. If you've ever tried a particular strategy, how did it work for you? (past experiences)

2. What obstacles might get in the way of you using this strategy more often now? (obstacles)

3. How or where could you use this strategy more often? (use it more)

Key Concept: Manage your stress.

(Note: I know these next strategies are all kind of obvious and much easier said than done, but it can be helpful to be reminded of them. They're worth working towards, even if we never get them perfect.)

U T *Manage your overall stress level.* Everyone is more reactive when they feel stressed out and overwhelmed. To the extent that you can, try to limit how many demands you have pressing on you at any one time.

Past experiences: _____

Obstacles: _____

Use it More: _____

Emotional Self-Control: Having Feelings Without Acting on Them

U T *Try to avoid over-committing yourself.* Everything seems interesting until we have too much going on. You can minimize those crunch-time stress reactions by taking less on and by graciously bowing out of some commitments when necessary (and with enough warning).

Past experiences: _____

Obstacles: _____

Use it More: _____

U T *Get enough sleep.* A good night's sleep makes everything easier. We are generally more positive and also less reactive when we've gotten enough sleep.

Past experiences: _____

Obstacles: _____

Use it More: _____

U T *Exercise regularly.* Exercise is a great stress reliever. It doesn't matter how you exercise, as long as you do it regularly. Even doing a set of push-ups or going for a quick walk around the block can clear your head.

Past experiences: _____

Obstacles: _____

Use it More: _____

U T *Make time for yourself.* It's easy to always feel behind, so it's important to set some time aside for yourself to do something purely for entertainment. If you don't recharge the batteries, you will burn out.

Past experiences: _____

Obstacles: _____

Use it More: _____

U T *Treat co-occurring anxiety and depression.* Adults with ADHD are more likely to be anxious and depressed (that one's pretty easy to figure out). Untreated, this may make your emotional control worse, so you may need to address these professionally, as well.

Past experiences: _____

Obstacles: _____

Use it More: _____

Key Concept: The less strongly you feel an emotion, the easier it is to control it.

U   T   *Try to avoid emotionally-provoking situations when possible.* Everyone has situations where they're more likely to have a strong reaction. It's much more work to calm a strong reaction than it is to avoid it in the first place (e.g., avoiding talking about politics with certain friends). To the extent that you can avoid it, don't go looking for trouble. Sometimes prevention is the best strategy. This doesn't mean that you should avoid every uncomfortable or difficult situation, but rather that some situations simply aren't worth the potential trouble.

Past experiences: _____

Obstacles: _____

Use it More: _____

U   T   *Prime yourself to step back from a situation before reacting.* If you're going into a situation that you know will be stressful or evoke some strong feelings, create a plan ahead of time for how to respond, rather than figuring it out in the moment. Think about how you can respond to different things the other person might do, as well as what outcomes you hope to achieve. Review that plan right before you go into the situation and then keep it in the front of your mind during the situation. If possible, bring in some written notes.

Past experiences: _____

Obstacles: _____

Use it More: _____

U   T   *Take a break.* If your two choices are to blow up or walk away, it's always better to walk away. Even just five seconds may be enough to help you calm down and re-gather yourself. Tell the other person that you are coming back so that she doesn't pursue you and continue the emotional discussion. If this is someone you have an ongoing relationship with (family member, friend, coworker), then explain to him/her that these breaks help you collect your thoughts and lead to a better outcome for everyone so the person is more likely to let you go.

Past experiences: _____

Obstacles: _____

Use it More: _____

U   T   *Take a mental break.* If you can't physically remove yourself from the situation, take a mental break. Consciously and intentionally shift your thinking to some other topic that is less emotional. It's better to shift your attention to something rather than away from something (e.g., "don't think about what a jerk he is."). Once you feel cooled off, then re-enter the conversation.

Past experiences: _____

Obstacles: _____

Use it More: _____

Emotional Self-Control: Having Feelings Without Acting on Them

U T *Consciously remind yourself of the bigger picture.* When you find yourself getting carried away with a feeling, try to pause and consider factors outside of the immediate situation. For example, if you get excited about going out to eat at one of your favorite restaurants, pause for a moment to think about whether you have the money and if there is anything else that you need to get done tonight.

Past experiences: _____

Obstacles: _____

Use it More: _____

U T *Consciously remind yourself of the other person's perspective.* We react to other people's actions, especially people we are closest to. This can happen very quickly when one person feels strongly. As much as we all like to think that we're justified in our feelings, there are times when we react strongly to someone for reasons that have little to do with that person. For example, if you know your romantic partner had a bad day at work, keep that in the front of your mind when she is being snappy so that you can hold back your initial defensive response. It comes down to not taking things personally that have little to do with you. This is a great skill to practice because it will make your relationships much smoother and more enjoyable.

Past experiences: _____

Obstacles: _____

Use it More: _____

U T *Train others to talk you down.* If you know you tend to get emotional in certain situations (e.g., political discussions, sales at certain stores), train some of your family and friends on how to talk to you (and how not to) about the bigger picture or another person's perspective so that you can catch yourself earlier in the process of getting caught up in a feeling.

Past experiences: _____

Obstacles: _____

Use it More: _____

U T *Walk it off.* If you have a really strong feeling, physical activity can help to dissipate it. This could be as simple as a walk around the building at work or doing a set of push-ups. Going for a run or to the gym or doing an exercise video also work really well if you have the time.

Past experiences: _____

Obstacles: _____

Use it More: _____

U   T *This too shall pass.* Remind yourself that, no matter how strongly you feel right now, the feeling will fade. This could be a positive feeling like being excited over a potential purchase or a negative feeling like being depressed over a date that went badly. Mentally talk yourself away from feeling consumed by the emotion. You still have the feeling, but part of you knows that you will feel differently, probably rather quickly.

Past experiences: _____

Obstacles: _____

Use it More: _____

U   T *Work on separating feeling from acting.* Our emotions often drive our behavior, but there doesn't necessarily need to be a direct connection between the two. Although it's easier said than done, it's possible to notice the feeling that you're having and what it makes you want to do without acting on it. Mindfulness training of various kinds teaches people how to do this.

Past experiences: _____

Obstacles: _____

Use it More: _____

Key Concept: Own up to your reactions.

U   T *Recognize that you have strong feelings and need to manage them more actively.* This is a part of who you are and can either serve you well or get you into trouble, so it's worth noting. By keeping in mind your tendency to have strong reactions, you can make better choices about the situations into which you put yourself.

Past experiences: _____

Obstacles: _____

Use it More: _____

U   T *Educate others to not make too much of your initial reaction.* Explain to family members, close friends, and perhaps some coworkers that your initial reaction tends to be stronger than other people's but that you settle down rather quickly and can then have a more productive discussion. This helps them not to overreact to your reaction so that you can wind up with a better outcome for everyone. You may also want to coach them on how you would like them to respond to you when you do have a strong emotional reaction.

Past experiences: _____

Obstacles: _____

Use it More: _____

Emotional Self-Control: Having Feelings Without Acting on Them

U T *Learn to give good apologies.* This is a good skill for everyone to practice, but it's especially helpful if you sometimes say things you don't really mean or if things come out wrong. If you can't prevent the reaction in the first place, the next best thing is to take ownership of it and clean up the fall-out. This will reduce the lingering side effects, especially when you have an ongoing relationship with someone. A good apology can also reduce your own shame or guilt afterwards—a little shame and guilt goes a long way.

Past experiences: _____

Obstacles: _____

Use it More: _____

U T *After you cool off, explain what you really meant.* If something came out wrong or if you said something that you didn't really mean, explain to the person what your rationale was and what you really meant. Don't deny what the other person perceived but show how you had better intentions than might have been conveyed.

Past experiences: _____

Obstacles: _____

Use it More: _____

Your Own Emotional Self-Control Strategies

There's a lot to be learned from past experiences. If it worked once, it might work again. Perhaps you kind of drifted away from a habit that was actually pretty good. Maybe you got bored with it. Maybe your habit got interrupted and you never came back to it. It happens. So maybe you just need to blow the dust off and use it again.

Think back on your past experiences over the years. What strategies have you used that have been helpful in making the most of your emotional self-control? Even though no strategy works perfectly, there had to be some that you used that were helpful and increased your batting average. And if they were helpful, they were probably consistent with the strategies that make the most of people's emotional self-control. Understanding how that works makes it more likely that you can apply them effectively to future challenges.

So let's identify those good strategies, understand how they are based in how your emotional self-control functions, and then apply them forward. It might be helpful to think about how a particular strategy fits into the key concepts for emotional self-control strategies, so I've included them below, as well. We'll answer the same questions that we did above.

Under each key concept, write out:

1. What strategy did you use?

2. How did this strategy work for you in the past?

3. What obstacles might get in the way of you using this strategy more often now?

4. How or where could you use this strategy more often?

107

Key Concept: Manage your stress.

Strategy: _____

Past Experiences: _____

Obstacles: _____

Use it More: _____

Strategy: _____

Past Experiences: _____

Obstacles: _____

Use it More: _____

Key Concept: The less strongly you feel an emotion, the easier it is to control it.

Strategy: _____

Past Experiences: _____

Obstacles: _____

Use it More: _____

Strategy: _____

Past Experiences: _____

Obstacles: _____

Use it More: _____

Key Concept: Own up to your reactions.

Strategy: _____

Past Experiences: _____

Obstacles: _____

Use it More: _____

Emotional Self-Control: Having Feelings Without Acting on Them

Strategy: _____

Past Experiences: _____

Obstacles: _____

Use it More: _____

Apply Your Strategies

Choose Your Targeted Strategies

Look back at the suggested strategies and your own strategies from above. Choose one to three strategies to work on first—pick a manageable number so you can do it well. You may want to look back at the section on Fallout from Emotional Self-Control Weaknesses (page 100) and match your strategies to your struggles.

Although it's tempting to jump headfirst into the deep end and start with the places that you're struggling the most, it may be worth getting your feet wet on some smaller and more manageable struggles first. These easier successes will teach you some helpful lessons that you can use when tackling the thornier problems. There's also nothing like success as a motivator.

★ Write down which strategies you are planning to try first:

1. _____

2. _____

3. _____

It's better to focus on just a few changes first. Once you have these down, come back and add in some other strategies.

4. _____

5. _____

6. _____

7. _____

8. _____

Create Opportunities to Practice

Practice makes perfect. Or at least better. Although it's likely that your life will throw you plenty of opportunities to apply these new strategies, it can also be helpful to intentionally create or anticipate situations to practice these strategies.

Strategy: _This too shall pass_

When and where can I apply this strategy? _When I feel something really strongly, like anger or when I really want to go do something, think about how I'll feel in a few minutes or an hour—not as strongly_

How do I know that this strategy is working? _I'm less pulled by feelings in the moment and make better choices_

Strategy: _____

When and where can I apply this strategy? _____

How do I know that this strategy is working? _____

Strategy: _____

When and where can I apply this strategy? _____

How do I know that this strategy is working? _____

Strategy: _____

When and where can I apply this strategy? _____

How do I know that this strategy is working? _____

Make the Commitment

Once you have your targeted strategies identified, you need to make a commitment to apply them. A strategy is only as good as your commitment. Because this is a workbook, you only have yourself to answer to (which is ultimately all you have even when someone else is involved). I can guarantee that the strategies in this book, and probably most of the strategies you come up with, are good ones. They will get the job done. It all comes down to using them.

So I encourage you to take the pledge below. But don't do this lightly—think about it. Maybe take a day or a week to think about it. If you're going to do this, give it your best effort. You deserve it.

My Pledge

I want a better life, so I commit to:

- Taking chances and trying something new.

- Doing my best to use these strategies diligently, even when I don't feel like it.

- Being open to learning from these experiences.

- Being flexible when a strategy isn't working.

- Only abandoning a strategy when I can replace it with another strategy that may work better.

_____

Signature   Date

See the Rewards

We're more likely to start and maintain behaviors that are being rewarded, so let's talk about those all-important rewards. They come in a number of different shapes and sizes, so let's not miss any—the more rewards, the better.

Automatic Rewards

Some rewards are directly tied to our behavior. For example:

- *Inherent feelings of satisfaction/pride.* Even if no one else notices, we notice and feel good about having done something well.

- *Natural consequences.* These are rewards that come from the world around us, like when someone offers a compliment. Or getting a good seat at the movies by showing up early.

It may be helpful to make a point of looking for and noticing these rewards. The hectic pace of life makes it easy to miss them—which then makes it easier to drop off from those good habits, even when they're working. Since you're more likely to find what you're actively looking for, let's identify what these rewards would be.

If I used these strategies diligently, I would feel:

_____

_____

_____

_____

_____

_____

_____

_____

If I used these strategies diligently, I would expect these natural consequences:

_____

_____

_____

_____

_____

_____

_____

_____

_____

Reward Yourself

Sometimes the inherent rewards and natural consequences aren't enough to push us over the edge to do something. This is when self-administered rewards come in handy. For example, "I will let myself do some actual woodworking after I clean up my shop." Or "I can check the sports scores after I finish these work emails."

Sometimes the reward is a good thing, whereas at other times the reward is just less bad than the first task. For example, "I will read this magazine article after I finish that technical report." Starting with the less desirable task creates an incentive to get to the more desirable task.

Think about some rewards that you can put in place for using your strategies. The reward needs to be good enough that it is actually motivating (but not so good that you'll skip the work and just take the reward).

If I use these strategies consistently, I will earn these rewards:

_____

_____

_____

_____

_____

_____

_____

_____

_____

_____

Fine-tune Your Approach

Learn from Setbacks

You may find that it's much harder than you thought to apply your targeted strategies and make progress on the struggles that you first decided to focus on. This is normal and often expectable. Life is a constant process of trying things and learning from the feedback. If you get stuck, take a few moments to think about it and learn some valuable lessons.

Why was this harder than I expected?

_____

_____

_____

_____

_____

_____

_____

_____

_____

What obstacles are getting in my way?

_____

_____

_____

_____

_____

_____

_____

_____

What lessons have I learned from this?

_____

_____

_____

_____

_____

_____

_____

_____

_____

What would need to change in order to make it worth attempting this again?

_____

Emotional Self-Control: Having Feelings Without Acting on Them

_____

_____

_____

_____

_____

_____

_____

_____

_____

How can I apply these lessons to my next efforts?

_____

_____

_____

_____

_____

_____

_____

_____

_____

_____

Based on these lessons, what would be a good area to focus on next?

_____

_____

_____

_____

_____

_____

_____

_____

_____

_____

The Big Picture: Refine Your Approach

As we talked about in Chapter 3: Reality-Based Motivation, we learn from our experiences and apply those lessons forward. Life is a constant learning process. Now that you've been applying your targeted strategies for a few days or weeks, what lessons have you learned? If you take a few moments, I guarantee you will come up with some productive ideas, even if you've already done this a few times in other chapters. As you keep moving through the workbook, you will continue to figure out new things.

Lessons learned about my strategies:

_____

_____

_____

_____

_____

_____

_____

_____

_____

Lessons learned about how my brain works:

_____

_____

_____

_____

_____

_____

_____

Emotional Self-Control: Having Feelings Without Acting on Them

_____

_____

_____

Lessons learned about how I motivate myself:

_____

_____

_____

_____

_____

_____

_____

_____

_____

Lessons learned about my workplace:

_____

_____

_____

_____

_____

_____

_____

_____

_____

_____

Make Your Life Better

Lessons learned about my home life:

_____

_____

_____

_____

_____

_____

_____

_____

_____

Lessons learned about using this workbook:

_____

_____

_____

_____

_____

_____

_____

_____

_____

CHAPTER 10

SELF-ACTIVATION: STARTING THEN FINISHING

What Self-Activation Is

When we're kids the various adults in our lives help us get going on tasks such as doing homework, getting dressed, and doing chores. You know, all that boring stuff that we don't really want to do and wish that magic elves would just do for us. With age, we're gradually expected to get ourselves going more and more and to manage our own obligations and deadlines.

The pressure we feel to start a task comes from the world around us as well as from within us—what I call external pressure and internal pressure. *External pressure* comes from other people, deadlines, rewards, punishments, and the situation in which we find ourselves. A report that is due tomorrow has much more external pressure than one that is due in a month. A boss who is breathing down your neck creates greater external pressure than a boss who says nothing. Everyone is more likely to start tasks with high external pressure. External pressure builds as a deadline approaches or as rewards or punishments increase.

Internal pressure is motivation that comes from within us, that is self-generated (i.e., the executive function of self-activation). It's easy to get going on things that we enjoy because the positive experiences of the situation reinforce our continued activity. We're having fun, so we keep going. In this way, our continued activity is partially externally motivated because of the enjoyment we get from the experience, so it's less about internal motivation. I often say that self-activating for enjoyable activities is like riding a bike downhill—it doesn't take much effort.

People tend to prefer to work towards rewards than to avoid punishments. Avoiding, minimizing, or escaping a negative situation can be effective in getting someone going, but it's not very inspiring. It's more motivating to work towards something positive like an "A" on a paper, recognition at work, or the appreciation of a romantic partner. Unfortunately, life tends to offer a variety of both situations. For example, people pay their electric bill on time because they want to avoid the negative situation of having their power cut off, followed by the even more negative situation of having to pay extra to turn it back on (even though it was the electric company who turned it off). While technically we could spin this that people pay the bill in order to gain the positive experience of continued electricity most people don't feel it that way, so paying bills feels more like a chore rather than an opportunity for a reward.

Success in life often requires the ability to complete all sorts of uninteresting tasks on a pretty regular basis. This means not just starting things, but also finishing most of them. Unfortunately, there are many situations where life doesn't give partial credit for things that are only partially done (e.g., the IRS isn't much impressed by a mostly finished tax return that is sitting on your desk).

Identify Your Struggles

Good solutions begin with a clear understanding of the problem. We'll begin here by listing the ways that self-activation weaknesses tend to affect someone's day to day life. You will then have some room to write other ways that your self-activation affects your life. Having this all in one place will make it easier to prioritize which areas to focus on first when we get to the strategies section.

Fallout from Self-Activation Weaknesses

Especially for boring tasks, people with ADHD have a hard time mustering up that internal pressure. They may think about it occasionally, but they just won't hit that tipping point where they can get themselves going to start or finish a task. This has social repercussions because people assume all sorts of negative character traits for people with ADHD and others who can't get themselves going reliably—lazy, self-indulgent, or irresponsible. (Any of these sound familiar?)

The irony, of course, is that most of these activities aren't really that hard, in and of themselves. It's not like people with ADHD don't have the skills to handle these tasks. For example, doing laundry, paying bills, and filing papers aren't inherently difficult—fighting the boredom is the hard part. Before a diagnosis, though, it can lead to accusations from oneself or others that these activities are easy, so the person should just do it.

Since people with ADHD aren't as good at generating that internal pressure for boring tasks, they are more dependent on external pressure. This means that they benefit from looming deadlines or an immediate reward or punishment. Far-off consequences just don't get them going because there isn't much external pressure yet.

The trick is to fire up that internal pressure and self-activating for things that aren't fun. That's more like riding a bike uphill—it takes intentional effort because the task itself doesn't offer much reward for continued activity. Of course, this is true for everyone. It's just that for people with ADHD, that hill is much steeper on the boring stuff, so it takes a much greater force of will to stick to them all the way through. This means that ADHD folks get more mentally tired from doing boring jobs and are therefore more likely to take a break sooner. Meanwhile, those fun distractions have much steeper downhills, so it's easy to slide off into a detour rather than trudge ahead.

For people with ADHD the difference between the downhills and the uphills is much greater than it is for people without ADHD. Unfortunately, a lot of the family members, friends, and coworkers of people with ADHD often don't understand this and take the attitude that the ADHD person should "just bite the bullet and get it done," not realizing that it isn't that easy. If it were, they would just do it. (Why would someone make their life harder if they didn't have to?) Since their ability to self-generate motivation is weak, external pressure helps those with ADHD not only start something but also push themselves through to the end. By analogy, you'll probably pedal harder up the hill if a big dog is chasing you.

Once a task is started, it also needs to be finished—all the way through to the end. And then all the materials should probably be put away. Although there are some people in the world who take great joy in checking completed items off of their to-do lists, most people with ADHD would rather just walk away once a task has lost its shine. As a result, it takes an extra mental push to finish something all the way to the very end because the task has become monotonous.

Adding to whatever brain-based difficulties with self-activation that people with ADHD may have, their history of struggles and setbacks (despite good effort) makes them more likely to expect more negative outcomes even if they were to apply themselves. So this creates a self-fulfilling prophecy where they don't bother to get going early and put in a good effort because it feels pointless. As a result, there is a feedback loop where past failures fuel current doubts and reduced effort. So ADHD struggles in the past also contribute to current avoidance.

I have a saying that the neurological drives the psychological—troubles with self-activation create a pessimistic mindset, which leads to further troubles with self-activation. So for many adults with ADHD, the psychological fall-out from living with ADHD creates a double-whammy where psychological reasons mimic and exacerbate weaknesses in this executive function. Of course this all becomes tangled together, so it's difficult to know whether someone is avoiding starting something for purely neurological reasons or if there is also some psychological choice involved. We might need a philosopher to help us sort that one out!

If you feel like the psychological reasons of avoidance and pessimism affect your ability to self-activate, you may want to take a look at Chapter 3: Reality-Based Motivation. The neurological and the psychological are both equally important.

It's worth noting here that in order to get going on a task, we first need to remember to do it. Unfortunately, as discussed in the chapters on working memory and prospective memory, people with ADHD struggle with the not-so-simple act of remembering what needs to be done. They're more likely to forget a future obligation, even if it is only a few seconds later. ("I'll do that as soon as I finish this.") Although this affects their ability to start tasks, it's really more about prospective memory than self-activation, since they never get to the point of engaging (or not) the executive function of self-activation. Once the person is actively thinking about a task, then it does become a matter of self-activation. This is one of the many ways that the executive functions interact and depend on each other as we navigate our complex world.

Weaknesses in self-activation tend to create common and predictable struggles in daily life. For example:

■ *Procrastination.* People who aren't good at generating internal pressure to start tasks are more dependent on external pressure. This often takes the form of waiting until the deadline is right on top of them. That last-minute pressure gets them going and provides the focus that their weak internal pressure just can't. Even if they were to start a task early, it often feels like they just fritter around with it because they can't fully harness their best efforts.

■ *Self-fulfilling prophecy: sense of dread beforehand, then panic in the moment.* Somewhere between feeling unconcerned about a long-off deadline and actually getting going on it, there is a building feeling of anxiety and activation that spurs the person into action. A habit of waiting too long before starting tasks tends to create a last-minute panic when the person finally does jump into frenzied activity. Although it may get the job done, this scramble can be a miserable experience, especially as unplanned obstacles pop up and shoot the person's (or other people's) anxiety through the roof. Once this pattern is established it can be even harder to make oneself start something because it feels better to avoid this negative experience as long as possible. Of course this avoidance just makes the experience even worse because there is even less margin for error, so it's even more stressful.

■ *Self-fulfilling prophecy: reduced quality when something is done quickly.* Racing through something at the last moment tends to interfere with doing one's best work. However, because of these difficulties with self-activation, many people with ADHD may not believe that they can get themselves going earlier, so they don't even try. This leaves them stuck with whatever they can whip up at the last minute. They may even assume that the low quality work is due to a lack of ability, rather than to racing through it, so there's little to be gained by taking longer since the quality won't be any better anyway. Of course, because there are times when the pressure of the last minute does provide a sense of focus and the person is able to do good work, these successes make it easy to justify always waiting to the last minute. Unfortunately, just because something works sometimes doesn't mean that it will work all the time or that a different approach wouldn't yield better results overall.

■ *Self-fulfilling prophecy: self-esteem protection.* It can feel safer to throw something together at the last minute and hope for the best. If it doesn't work out well, the person can defend herself by saying that it wasn't her best effort. ("Of course it wasn't very good—I did it in like twenty minutes.") There's more ego on the line and exposure to real criticism when we put in good effort and the outcome isn't good enough. Sloppy effort offers a plausible escape from any criticism, whether it comes from others or from our own critical voices.

■ *Nag magnets.* Because their procrastination makes other people nervous ("You haven't started that yet?!"), they tend to get nagged a lot as the other people attempt to reduce their own building internal pressure and anxiety about the looming deadline. In order to make themselves feel less anxious, the person without ADHD begins applying external pressure upon the ADHD person (a.k.a. "reminding" and "encouraging" which is a.k.a. "nagging" and "annoying").

■ *Get resentfully bailed out.* If the person with ADHD waits too long to start a task, someone else may jump in and just do the task himself for fear that otherwise it won't be done at all. While this does indeed help the non-ADHD person feel less anxious about the looming deadline, he may also resent having to do it, even if no one asked him to do so. Similarly, the person with ADHD perhaps feels guilty for being bailed out again. This can create messy relationship dynamics where no one wins.

■ *Feel incompetent.* Related to the prior point, getting bailed out too often can also strengthen a belief in both people that the ADHD person isn't capable of getting things done and needs to be rescued. At its worst, it can create a sense of entitlement where the person with ADHD expects others to handle her responsibilities and the other person enables this behavior by over-functioning.

■ *Seen as self-indulgent or irresponsible.* Other people may see the person with ADHD self-activate pretty easily for enjoyable activities but not for boring obligations. The non-ADHD person therefore might see it as a matter of choice and become resentful about having to pick up the slack on the boring jobs. This is where those negative assumptions about character traits come in. The thing is, for people with ADHD, this is usually more about brain-based low internal pressure than it is about character. I wrote about how to improve the dynamics that often occur when one person in a relationship has ADHD in chapter 15 of my prior book *More Attention, Less Deficit: Success Strategies for Adults with ADHD*.

■ *Less likely to work towards long-term gains.* Consequences that are too far away don't have as much gravitational pull on the actions of people with ADHD as do more immediate rewards or punishments.

As a result they tend to spend most of their time on activities with more immediate feedback, so longer-term projects tend to get squeezed out and not worked on. This can have significant effects on the achievement of major goals, such as getting a degree or certification, sticking with a job long enough to be promoted, saving for retirement, getting into shape, etc.

- *Too often motivated by the avoidance of punishment.* Related to the prior point, if long-term goals don't spur people with ADHD into action, they tend to spend too much time putting out fires with more immediate situations. Reacting to the crisis of the moment can certainly add some excitement to one's day, but it tends to not leave a lingering feeling of satisfaction with a job well done. Instead, it feels like getting lucky with a bunch of narrow misses.

- *Miss deadlines when start too late.* The closer a deadline is, the more vulnerable we are to unexpected setbacks. Some setbacks, obstacles, or delays can be predictable, whereas others are unexpected (e.g., power outages, computer malfunctions, illness, etc.). Starting later shrinks that cushion of extra time to deal with things that arise, so it's more likely that the deadline will be missed.

- *Never start a task.* Although many tasks eventually result in some external pressure if we don't start them quickly enough, many tasks can be ignored for a long time or forever. For example, by never getting around to re-evaluating their car insurance policy options, people with ADHD may pay extra for years by carrying too much insurance.

- *Lots of partially completed tasks.* They may start something but not quite get it all the way finished. This is partially because that they don't feel a strong sense of satisfaction with putting on the finishing touches, but probably also because they got distracted and pulled onto something else first.

Hang in There!

We've now identified some of the difficulties that can come from a weak self-activation. It's important to identify the problems before getting into solutions. You may feel worse now because you're more aware of your struggles (and maybe even discovered some problems you didn't realize you had!). You may feel discouraged at this point if you feel like you have more problems than solutions. Hang in there! We'll get to the solutions next.

Identify Your Strategies

Let's now take a look at potential strategies to address these self-activation struggles. This is where things begin to get better.

Some people have more struggles at work or school, while others have more challenges at home. Each of these parts of your life places different demands on you and also offers different supports, so you may perform really well in one but barely hold it together in the other. Because of this potential difference, you may find it helpful to practice new strategies more in one setting than in the other.

Or you may find that you have some of the same struggles in both situations. If this is the case, some of the same strategies may work in both places. This will provide some helpful carry-over benefit from practicing the same strategies throughout your day. You may also find that some strategies work better in one situation than in the other simply because the two situations are too different from each other. Do whatever works best.

The goal here is to go through the process of identifying targeted strategies based on your strengths, weaknesses, and what you need to get done. Some strategies will just be a better fit for you. Like many other situations in life, you're more likely to arrive at the best solutions if you follow a good process of evaluating your options. This will take some work, but it will be worth it. Also, because you're going to do it step by step, it should feel more manageable and less overwhelming and be more productive.

Self-Activation Strategies Key Concepts

Most of the strategies that make the most of your self-activation will fall under one of these basic ideas. By simplifying all those other strategies down to three basic ideas, it's easier to learn the concepts and apply them later.

- Make the first step smaller and more manageable.

- Visualize the rewards for starting and/or finishing (and create some if necessary).

- Work on the task even if you don't feel motivated.

Suggested Self-Activation Strategies

Let's start things off with a list of strategies that tend to be helpful for self-activation weaknesses so you can see where we're going. Some of these strategies may jump out at you—good!

Circle the **U** in the margin next to the strategies that you have used in the past and circle the **T** next to the ones that you haven't used before but think you might benefit from trying.

After each suggested strategy, write out:

1. If you've ever tried a particular strategy, how did it work for you? (past experiences)

2. What obstacles might get in the way of you using this strategy more often now? (obstacles)

3. How or where could you use this strategy more often? (use it more)

Key concept: Make the first step smaller and more manageable.

U T *Set it up.* An easy way to create some momentum on a task is to set things up by gathering the necessary information or supplies, getting directions, determining the end result you're going for, etc. Then when the time comes to start it, you're ready to go. For example, if you need to paint the bathroom, buy the paint, gather your brushes and rollers, and put everything near the bathroom. The set up usually doesn't take very long but it gives you a sense of momentum and makes it easier to jump into the task itself.

Past experiences: _____

Obstacles: _____

Use it More: _____

U   T *Set a timer.* Commit to working on the task for a certain amount of time—even just five minutes. A short period of time doesn't feel too horrible and is easier to commit to for most people. This can create a sense of momentum where you then keep at it or at least have an easier time coming back to the task later.

Past experiences: _____

Obstacles: _____

Use it More: _____

U   T *Set a stopping point.* Sometimes it's better to start with a certain piece of a task—for example, dealing just with the clothes on the floor, clearing off your desk, looking at three vacation websites, etc. This can feel more manageable than having to commit to the entire task.

Past experiences: _____

Obstacles: _____

Use it More: _____

U   T *Break a big project into multiple smaller steps.* Sometimes the first step in a big project is to create a plan for how to do it in multiple pieces. For example, doing your taxes involves gathering all the necessary information, sorting it, adding it up, and entering it into the tax preparation software. You can then create a schedule for when each piece will be tackled. Each smaller step is less daunting than having to do the entire thing at one time.

Past experiences: _____

Obstacles: _____

Use it More: _____

U   T *Figure out what to do.* We tend to avoid tasks where we don't know what to do. If you're uncertain of what to do next, take some time to figure out what you need to do or how you need to do it. This may involve doing some research or talking to others to get some ideas. Be willing not to know and have some faith that you'll figure it out. Some tasks require a few attempts before we figure them out, so it's OK to feel stuck initially.

Past experiences: _____

Obstacles: _____

Use it More: _____

U T *Do tasks in clumps.* Since it can take some mental effort to shift gears, it can be helpful to group several of the same kind of task together (e.g., sending out emails, making shopping lists, doing online research, etc.). This way you can move through several items on your to-do list quickly before switching to something else. It's especially helpful if you can combine several tasks into one trip, whether it's shopping or stopping by a colleague's office.

Past experiences: _____

Obstacles: _____

Use it More: _____

Key concept: Visualize the rewards for finishing (and create some if necessary).

U T *Think about the rewards and punishments as vividly as possible.* We naturally shrink the intensity of future rewards and punishments because we feel the more immediate rewards and punishments more strongly (e.g., the fun of watching a favorite TV show now feels greater than the pain of staying up late tonight to finish a report). You can counterbalance this by intentionally playing up those future positive or negative feelings and by downplaying the current feelings. This will make it more likely that you will get yourself going now on what you should be doing, rather than allow yourself to do something more fun.

Past experiences: _____

Obstacles: _____

Use it More: _____

U T *Focus on the rewards, not the punishments.* Most tasks have both a reward for completion and a punishment for not doing them. Although the punishments may stand out more, try to focus on what is gained from doing them (e.g., loading the dishwasher gets you a calm evening at home, whereas not doing it creates a fight with your romantic partner). Earning rewards is more motivating than avoiding punishments.

Past experiences: _____

Obstacles: _____

Use it More: _____

U T *Make it more fun.* Turn on some music, call a friend, invite a friend over, put on a movie, or whatever will make the task more enjoyable. Just because you're doing something boring doesn't mean that you need to be totally bored.

Past experiences: _____

Obstacles: _____

Use it More: _____

U T *Create a reward when one doesn't otherwise exist.* Some tasks don't provide much of a reward for completing them. For example, unless you're getting a big refund, sending off your tax return isn't all that fun. In these cases, you may need to create your own reward to work towards. This could be something as small as allowing yourself to call a friend afterward.

Past experiences: _____

Obstacles: _____

Use it More: _____

U T *Shorten the wait for rewards or punishments.* A far-off reward or punishment doesn't affect our current behavior as much as something that is more immediate. (Why do you think most people are so bad at saving for retirement?) You can use this to your advantage by intentionally shortening the wait for a reward of punishment, for example, by creating a reward for starting and completing a part of a task, rather than having to wait until it's completely finished.

Past experiences: _____

Obstacles: _____

Use it More: _____

U T *Use your energy bursts productively.* When you feel alert and charged up, use that energy productively by tackling the more demanding tasks. This could be the tasks that you really don't feel like doing or it could be the tasks that require more focus and intense mental effort. Don't squander good energy on easy stuff.

Past experiences: _____

Obstacles: _____

Use it More: _____

U T *Remind yourself of how you would like to see yourself.* Most people like to think of themselves as diligent, responsible, and reliable. People with ADHD are no different. When you feel like procrastinating, remind yourself how your current actions affect how you see yourself. It's a matter of integrity.

Past experiences: _____

Obstacles: _____

Use it More: _____

Key concept: Work on the task even if you don't feel motivated.

U T *Just jump in.* We can get stuck when we don't know where to start or there are too many things to do. If there is no obvious first step, just jump in. Doing something (anything) is often better than doing nothing. This will also give you feedback and help you figure out what the best next step is, more than just thinking about it. There comes a point where more thinking just leads to running around the same circles inside our head, because we have no new information. Jumping in gives us new information, which helps us understand the situation better so we can make better-informed choices.

Past experiences: _____

Obstacles: _____

Use it More: _____

U T *Don't take other people's anxiety personally.* Nobody likes feeling pushed to do something. Not that it makes it any less annoying at the time, but try to remember that the person isn't trying to control you, he's just trying to control his own anxiety. As tempting and automatic as it is to push back when we're pushed, resist reflexively digging in your heels. There are times when the wisest thing to do is to hold the line when someone is pushing you, but this doesn't mean that it's always the smartest decision. If you're going to hold the line, do it for well thought-out reasons.

Past experiences: _____

Obstacles: _____

Use it More: _____

U T *Push others to manage their own anxiety.* In order to do this, you need to create a track record that shows that you do indeed get the job done. If you drop the ball too often or barely manage to scrape by at the last minute, you don't have much credibility to tell other people that they shouldn't worry. This credibility is earned, but it can create a real shift in the relationship when you do it.

Past experiences: _____

Obstacles: _____

Use it More: _____

U T *Test whether quality goes up from starting earlier.* If you feel that certain tasks don't work out well anyway even when you do start them earlier, run a science experiment—give it a try and see what happens. The results may surprise you.

Past experiences: _____

Obstacles: _____

Use it More: _____

U T *Separate motivation and action.* Although it's easier to get started on tasks that we are motivated for, it is possible to do things that we don't really feel like doing. It just takes more of a mental push to do so. We can't always magically call up our willpower, but there are times when biting the bullet actually works.

Past experiences: _____

Obstacles: _____

Use it More: _____

U T *Make good use of the low times.* When you're tired, distracted, or preoccupied you can still use that time productively by knocking out some easy or less boring tasks. This takes them off your plate so that you don't need to do them later.

Past experiences: _____

Obstacles: _____

Use it More: _____

U T *Kill the albatross.* Most people have a handful of tasks hanging over their heads that they wish were done but can never quite manage to make themselves accomplish. Think about how good it will feel to have them off your back, then commit some time to killing those albatrosses.

Past experiences: _____

Obstacles: _____

Use it More: _____

U T *Make a public commitment.* We can use social pressure in a good way by telling other people about our plans to accomplish something (e.g., run a 5 K, clean out the attic, etc.). Knowing that we may need to answer to these other people can be a tremendous motivator. You can even ask them to ask you about your project at a specified later point so that you have created a deadline.

Past experiences: _____

Obstacles: _____

Use it More: _____

U T *Dump the losers.* A busy life tends to create a full to-do list. Unfortunately more hours don't appear as the obligations pile up, so there comes a point where some tasks need to be dropped—they just didn't make the cut. If you decide that you're just never going to get to something, that it just isn't important enough, then dump it and don't look back. Keeping too many marginally-important tasks hanging around will just distract you from the more important ones. (And stress you out in the meantime.)

Past experiences: _____

Obstacles: _____

Use it More: _____

Your Own Self-Activation Strategies

There's a lot to be learned from past experiences. If it worked once, it might work again. Perhaps you kind of drifted away from a habit that was actually pretty good. Maybe you got bored with it. Maybe your habit got interrupted and you never came back to it. It happens. So maybe you just need to blow the dust off and use it again.

SECTION II   Make Your Life Better

Think back on your past experiences over the years. What strategies have you used that have been helpful in making the most of your self-activation? Even though no strategy works perfectly, there had to be some that you used that were helpful and increased your batting average. And if they were helpful, they were probably consistent with the strategies that make the most of people's self-activation. Understanding how that works makes it more likely that you can apply them effectively to future challenges.

So let's identify those good strategies, understand how they are based in how your self-activation functions, and then apply them forward. It might be helpful to think about how a particular strategy fits into the key concepts for self-activation strategies, so I've included them below, as well. We'll answer the same questions that we did above.

Under each key concept, write out:

1. What strategy did you use?

2. How did this strategy work for you in the past?

3. What obstacles might get in the way of you using this strategy more often now?

4. How or where could you use this strategy more often?

Key Concept: Make important stimuli stand out more to make it more likely that your attention will stay focused on them.

Strategy: _____

Past Experiences: _____

Obstacles: _____

Use it More: _____

Strategy: _____

Past Experiences: _____

Obstacles: _____

Use it More: _____

Key Concept: The fewer distractions, the easier it is to stay focused on and remember what you should.

Strategy: _____

Past Experiences: _____

Obstacles: _____

Use it More: _____

Strategy: _____

Past Experiences: _____

Obstacles: _____

Use it More: _____

Key Concept: Write things down rather than try to keep it all in your head.

Strategy: _____

Past Experiences: _____

Obstacles: _____

Use it More: _____

Strategy: _____

Past Experiences: _____

Obstacles: _____

Use it More: _____

Apply Your Strategies

Choose Your Targeted Strategies

Look back at the suggested strategies and your own strategies from above. Choose one to three strategies to work on first—pick a manageable number so you can do it well. You may want to look back at the section on Fallout from Self-Activation Weaknesses (page 120) and match your strategies to your struggles.

Although it's tempting to jump headfirst into the deep end and start with the places that you're struggling the most, it may be worth getting your feet wet on some smaller and more manageable struggles first. These easier successes will teach you some helpful lessons that you can use when tackling the thornier problems. There's also nothing like success as a motivator.

★ Write down which strategies you are planning to try first:

1. _____

2. _____

3. _____

It's better to focus on just a few changes first. Once you have these down, come back and add in some other strategies.

4. _____

5. _____

6. _____

7. _____

8. _____

Create Opportunities to Practice

Practice makes perfect. Or at least better. Although it's likely that your life will throw you plenty of opportunities to apply these new strategies, it can also be helpful to intentionally create or anticipate situations to practice these strategies.

Strategy: *Focus on the rewards, not punishments*

When and where can I apply this strategy? *When I feel like I'm doing something that just feels like a burden*

How do I know that this strategy is working? *I will feel better about doing things I don't really want to do. I will feel less like someone is making me do things*

Strategy: _____

When and where can I apply this strategy? _____

How do I know that this strategy is working? _____

Strategy: _____

When and where can I apply this strategy? _____

How do I know that this strategy is working? _____

Strategy: _____

When and where can I apply this strategy? _____

_____

How do I know that this strategy is working? _____

_____

Make the Commitment

Once you have your targeted strategies identified, you need to make a commitment to apply them. A strategy is only as good as your commitment. Because this is a workbook, you only have yourself to answer to (which is ultimately all you have even when someone else is involved). I can guarantee that the strategies in this book, and probably most of the strategies you come up with, are good ones. They will get the job done. It all comes down to using them.

So I encourage you to take the pledge below. But don't do this lightly—think about it. Maybe take a day or a week to think about it. If you're going to do this, give it your best effort. You deserve it.

My Pledge

I want a better life, so I commit to:

■ Taking chances and trying something new.

■ Doing my best to use these strategies diligently, even when I don't feel like it.

■ Being open to learning from these experiences.

■ Being flexible when a strategy isn't working.

■ Only abandoning a strategy when I can replace it with another strategy that may work better.

_____

Signature   Date

See the Rewards

We're more likely to start and maintain behaviors that are being rewarded, so let's talk about those all-important rewards. They come in a number of different shapes and sizes, so let's not miss any—the more rewards, the better.

Automatic Rewards

Some rewards are directly tied to our behavior. For example:

■ *Inherent feelings of satisfaction/pride.* Even if no one else notices, we notice and feel good about having done something well.

■ *Natural consequences.* These are rewards that come from the world around us, like when someone offers a compliment. Or getting a good seat at the movies by showing up early.

It may be helpful to make a point of looking for and noticing these rewards. The hectic pace of life makes it easy to miss them—which then makes it easier to drop off from those good habits, even when they're working. Since you're more likely to find what you're actively looking for, let's identify what these rewards would be.

If I used these strategies diligently, I would feel:

_____

_____

_____

_____

_____

_____

_____

_____

_____

_____

If I used these strategies diligently, I would expect these natural consequences:

_____

_____

_____

_____

_____

_____

_____

_____

_____

_____

Reward Yourself

Sometimes the inherent rewards and natural consequences aren't enough to push us over the edge to do something. This is when self-administered rewards come in handy. For example, "I will let myself do some actual woodworking after I clean up my shop." Or "I can check the sports scores after I finish these work emails."

Sometimes the reward is a good thing, whereas at other times the reward is just less bad than the first task. For example, "I will read this magazine article after I finish that technical report." Starting with the less desirable task creates an incentive to get to the more desirable task.

Think about some rewards that you can put in place for using your strategies. The reward needs to be good enough that it is actually motivating (but not so good that you'll skip the work and just take the reward).

If I use these strategies consistently, I will earn these rewards:

_____

_____

_____

_____

_____

_____

_____

_____

_____

_____

Fine-tune Your Approach

Learn from Setbacks

You may find that it's much harder than you thought to apply your targeted strategies and make progress on the struggles that you first decided to focus on. This is normal and often expectable. Life is a constant process of trying things and learning from the feedback. If you get stuck, take a few moments to think about it and learn some valuable lessons.

Why was this harder than I expected?

_____

_____

_____

_____

_____

_____

_____

_____

_____

What obstacles are getting in my way?

_____

_____

_____

_____

_____

_____

_____

_____

_____

_____

_____

What lessons have I learned from this?

_____

_____

_____

_____

_____

_____

_____
_____
_____
_____

What would need to change in order to make it worth attempting this again?

_____
_____
_____
_____
_____
_____
_____
_____
_____

How can I apply these lessons to my next efforts?

_____
_____
_____
_____
_____
_____
_____
_____
_____

Based on these lessons, what would be a good area to focus on next?

_____

_____

_____

_____

_____

_____

_____

_____

_____

_____

The Big Picture: Refine Your Approach

As we talked about in Chapter 3: Reality-Based Motivation, we learn from our experiences and apply those lessons forward. Life is a constant learning process. Now that you've been applying your targeted strategies for a few days or weeks, what lessons have you learned? If you take a few moments, I guarantee you will come up with some productive ideas, even if you've already done this a few times in other chapters. As you keep moving through the workbook, you will continue to figure out new things.

Lessons learned about my strategies:

_____

_____

_____

_____

_____

_____

_____

_____

_____

Lessons learned about how my brain works:

_____

_____

_____

_____

_____

_____

_____

_____

_____

Lessons learned about how I motivate myself:

_____

_____

_____

_____

_____

_____

_____

_____

_____

_____

_____

Lessons learned about my workplace:

_____

_____

_____

_____

_____
_____
_____
_____
_____

Lessons learned about my home life:

_____
_____
_____
_____
_____
_____
_____
_____
_____

Lessons learned about using this workbook:

_____
_____
_____
_____
_____
_____
_____
_____
_____

CHAPTER 11

HINDSIGHT AND FORETHOUGHT: USING THE PAST AND FUTURE TO GUIDE THE PRESENT

What Hindsight and Forethought Is

With age comes wisdom (hopefully). After going through an experience once or twice, ideally we learn something that we can use when a similar situation arises. Better yet, hopefully we can make predictions about a situation so that we can influence the outcome before anything actually happens. These abilities involve the two related executive functions of hindsight and forethought. *Hindsight* involves using lessons from the past to guide behavior in the present (a.k.a. wisdom). *Forethought* involves using projected future consequences to guide behavior in the present. We use forethought to look ahead to see likely challenges and think about what kinds of responses will probably work best. To predict the future accurately we have to be able to stop and evaluate current circumstances, think about how similar situations worked out in the past, mentally sort through our options, and choose the best one. So there's a lot going on here, even if it occurs in an instant.

Although they work closely together, hindsight looks backwards, whereas forethought looks forward. In both cases, the ultimate goal is the same, to create the best possible future by managing the interactions in the present most effectively.

We don't have to keep burning our hands on the stove to know that it will be hot and therefore to use an oven mitt. The same process occurs for much more complex situations, as we constantly shift our attention among the past, present, and future. The most effective decision-making takes all three equally into account. Focusing too much on the past makes someone insensitive to current nuances and therefore inflexible. Focusing too much on the present makes someone shortsighted and too likely to be influenced by the immediate situation. Focusing too much on the future diminishes the present moment and potentially creates an anxious paralysis.

Of course for hindsight and forethought to work well, we have to have a pretty good idea of what's going on so that we can prepare for the right situation. This involves both self-awareness as well as awareness of other people and outside events. Therefore, we have to monitor all of these internal and external events as they unfold so that we can plan and respond accordingly. To work well, this monitoring requires a gap between stimulus and response—we have to be able to take it all in and think about it before doing anything. This means not just reacting to the most obvious aspects of the situation but also considering the more subtle parts.

One of the hallmarks of maturity is strong hindsight and forethought. We expect adults to be able to think beyond the current moment and make choices that take the big picture into account and benefit their long-range interests. In fact, some of the most moralistic judgments are made about those who focus mostly on the present.

Identify Your Struggles

Good solutions begin with a clear understanding of the problem. We'll begin here by listing the ways that hindsight and forethought weaknesses tend to affect someone's day to day life. You will then have some room to write other ways that your hindsight and forethought affects your life. Having this all in one place will make it easier to prioritize which areas to focus on first when we get to the strategies section.

Fallout from Hindsight and Forethought Weaknesses

As with all the other executive functions, people with ADHD use their hindsight and forethought very well sometimes, but not always. They're inconsistent. Too often they get caught up in the situation and don't stop to access their knowledge. The struggle for most people with ADHD is to apply that wisdom in the heat of the moment. If you were to ask them beforehand how best to react, they could tell you. If you were to ask them afterward, they can tell you how they could have handled it better. Unfortunately, this knowledge doesn't translate reliably enough into doing the right thing at the right time. They know it, but they don't do it.

The snag occurs when they aren't able to use their hindsight to guide their actions in the moment. The reason is that we need to stop for a moment to think before acting in order to have time to bring back the lessons of those past experiences. This is that crucial pause I was talking about in Chapter 5: Response Inhibition. For too many people with ADHD, they've already leaped before looking and only afterward realize that they're in trouble. As a result, they're often in a position of having to explain why they did something that even they know wasn't such a good idea—why they bought something from the telemarketer without getting all the details or why they used a butter knife to tighten a loose screw. The problem is that there are no good explanations, since they know they made a bad decision. This leaves them with "I don't know. I just didn't think about it," which is actually pretty accurate. Maybe not satisfying, but accurate.

Another reason they make these less-than-ideal choices is that adult life involves lots of situations where we're faced with a choice that offers an immediate small reward but a larger punishment later. For example, staying up too late watching a movie is fun in the moment but painful the next day. Impulse buying is exciting at the time but problematic when the credit card bill arrives. As kids, we have adults around us who know these things and prevent us from making these kinds of choices. As adults, though, we're expected to be able to do this for ourselves, which is easier said than done for those with ADHD. When confronted with these tempting choices, ideally we can pause for a moment to activate our forethought to help us sort through our options before choosing. Because adults with ADHD don't pause as reliably they don't use their forethought as often, which means that they make more choices that benefit them in the moment but carry a higher price later.

Weaknesses in hindsight and forethought tend to create common and predictable struggles in daily life. For example:

- *Know how to create good plans but don't do it.* When they stop long enough to consider their options, people with ADHD can create good plans. They can also be very good at telling others how to handle situations but then don't follow their own advice. (Which can be baffling to themselves and others.) The problem is that they too often don't stop long enough to create a plan and then follow the plan they've created.

- *Fly by the seat of their pants.* Because they don't pause to think through what will happen and how to respond to likely events, they have to figure things out on the spot. This makes them more likely to make less optimal decisions than if they had had more time to think about it.

- *Forced to choose among fewer options.* Related to the above point, the earlier we address an issue, the more options we tend to have. Dealing with something at the last minute or in the heat of the moment tends to leave us with fewer options than if we had planned ahead more.

- *Trouble putting all the steps together.* Creating a multistep plan requires the person to think of all the necessary steps and then put them into the optimal order. People with ADHD are more likely to lose efficiency when they need to go back to a step they didn't plan for or forgot to include because they didn't think it all through in enough detail. Perhaps the classic example of this is the child who tells his parents at dinner that he has a science project due the next day, not figuring into his planning that he should have gotten supplies from the store earlier in the day or week. Parents love these moments.

- *Don't monitor the progress of their plans.* Once a plan has been created we need to adjust fluidly to the evolving circumstances. This involves the ability to sense when events are slipping away from us and changing course to get things back on track. In addition to drifting off onto unrelated activities, people with ADHD may not notice when it's time to change gears that things aren't going as they had initially planned. Something may be taking longer than expected or they may not be achieving the desired results. Noticing this requires that the person pause occasionally to lift his head up from the action and compare the current situation to the planned situation.

- *Lecture, lecture, lecture.* When people with ADHD do things that even they know better than, they make themselves easy targets for indignant, disappointed, or confused lectures. Although the feelings are easy to understand, the lectures don't tell people with ADHD anything that they don't already know.

- *Respond to only part of the situation.* When people with ADHD react too quickly they are more likely to respond to the more obvious aspects of the situation. This leaves them vulnerable to not considering other equally important, but less glaring, elements, for example, responding to an insulting comment with anger before recognizing that the speaker has been having a bad day and probably didn't mean to come across so harshly.

- *Repeat the same mistakes.* Even though they know better (especially the second time), because they don't stop to think about a situation before reacting, they're more likely to make the same mistake twice, or more. Once again, they didn't stop long enough to access their knowledge and make a different choice.

- *Reactive, chaotic, stressful lifestyle.* If they don't plan ahead and consider obstacles often enough, they will spend more time putting out fires and scrambling to make something work at the last minute. Of course this becomes a feedback loop because there is even less time and mental energy left to think about how to make the next situation a better one.

Hang in There!

We've now identified some of the difficulties that can come from a weak hindsight and forethought. It's important to identify the problems before getting into solutions. You may feel worse now because you're more aware of your struggles (and maybe even discovered some problems you didn't realize you had!). You may feel discouraged at this point if you feel like you have more problems than solutions. Hang in there! We'll get to the solutions next.

Identify Your Strategies

Let's now take a look at potential strategies to address these hindsight and forethought struggles. This is where things begin to get better.

Some people have more struggles at work or school, while others have more challenges at home. Each of these parts of your life places different demands on you and also offers different supports, so you may perform really well in one but barely hold it together in the other. Because of this potential difference, you may find it helpful to practice new strategies more in one setting than in the other.

Or you may find that you have some of the same struggles in both situations. If this is the case, some of the same strategies may work in both places. This will provide some helpful carry-over benefit from practicing the same strategies throughout your day. You may also find that some strategies work better in one situation than in the other simply because the two situations are too different from each other. Do whatever works best.

The goal here is to go through the process of identifying targeted strategies based on your strengths, weaknesses, and what you need to get done. Some strategies will just be a better fit for you. Like many other situations in life, you're more likely to arrive at the best solutions if you follow a good process of evaluating your options. This will take some work, but it will be worth it. Also, because you're going to do it step by step, it should feel more manageable and less overwhelming and be more productive.

Hindsight and Forethought Strategies Key Concepts

Most of the strategies that make the most of your hindsight and forethought will fall under one of these basic ideas. By simplifying all those other strategies down to three basic ideas, it's easier to learn the concepts and apply them later.

■ Intentionally pause before reacting and then consider your options.

■ Make a point of seeing how you're doing occasionally and then adjust as needed.

■ Reflect upon lessons learned.

Suggested Hindsight and Forethought Strategies

Let's start things off with a list of strategies that tend to be helpful for hindsight and forethought weaknesses so you can see where we're going. Some of these strategies may jump out at you—good!

Hindsight and Forethought: Using the Past and Future to Guide the Present

Circle the **U** in the margin next to the strategies that you have used in the past and circle the **T** next to the ones that you haven't used before but think you might benefit from trying.

After each suggested strategy, write out:

1. If you've ever tried a particular strategy, how did it work for you? (past experiences)

2. What obstacles might get in the way of you using this strategy more often now? (obstacles)

3. How or where could you use this strategy more often? (use it more)

Key Concept: Intentionally pause before reacting and then consider your options.

U T *Create a schedule for the day and week.* The act of planning out your time makes it more likely that you will use your hindsight and forethought than you would if you simply reacted to things in the moment. Although setting a schedule can feel constraining and involves some additional work to maintain, it also helps to reduce infiltration by less worthwhile activities that we will later regret.

Past experiences: _____

Obstacles: _____

Use it More: _____

U T *Schedule time to do specific tasks.* Many tasks don't have a specific time in which they need to happen (e.g., bills could be paid in the morning or at night). These items therefore often get squeezed out by other tasks that do have a specific time (e.g., meetings, a TV show) or events happening in the moment (e.g., a ringing phone, a coworker who stops by). By putting these tasks into your schedule at a specific time you have made it more likely that you will get to them and are therefore using good forethought.

Past experiences: _____

Obstacles: _____

Use it More: _____

U T *Regularly think ahead to what is coming up in your day or week and how you want to handle each situation.* It's best to have a designated time, like first thing at work, so that you know that this planning time will happen. But you can also use other random moments through your day, such as when driving or waiting for a meeting to start. This is an intentional process of thinking ahead about likely situations, priorities/preferences, potential obstacles, how you will react, etc.

Past experiences: _____

Obstacles: _____

Use it More: _____

U T *Don't commit to anything without checking your schedule first.* Check to make sure that you actually have the time available. This of course requires you always to have your schedule with you. If you don't have your schedule, write a note or ask the person to email you a reminder, saying, "I might be able to do this, but need to check my schedule first. I'll let you know if I can do it."

Past experiences: _____

Obstacles: _____

Use it More: _____

U T *Talk it through.* Talking through our plans with someone else can help us fill in the blanks that we hadn't considered. The process of telling someone else pushes us to think about the details that we might otherwise skip past and assume will work out well. You could talk to a romantic partner, friend, coworker, boss, therapist, coach, organizer, mentor, etc. Even talking to your dog could be helpful if you make the time to do it.

Past experiences: _____

Obstacles: _____

Use it More: _____

U T *Avoid or minimize situations where you tend to react impulsively.* If you know you tend to leap before looking in certain situations, it's usually easier to not put yourself into the situation than it is to do the better thing once you are there. For example, it's probably easier to not even turn on the TV in the morning than it is to pull yourself away when it's time to leave for work.

Past experiences: _____

Obstacles: _____

Use it More: _____

U T *Create a budget.* It's easier to judge how worthy a particular expenditure is if you have a budget. Otherwise it's just mental guesswork as to whether you should spend the money, which makes it too likely that you will discover once it's too late that you shouldn't have spent it.

Past experiences: _____

Obstacles: _____

Use it More: _____

Hindsight and Forethought: Using the Past and Future to Guide the Present

Key Concept: *Make a point of occasionally seeing how you're doing and then adjust as needed.*

U   T   *Plan check-in breaks.* When creating a plan for how to handle a situation, build in specific times or progress points to assess how you're doing and whether a change of tack is necessary. These should be natural break points, such as when returning from lunch or after having laid the first row of tiles. If you have a written schedule or plan, write these breaks down. If you're running through the plan mentally, remind yourself frequently about the breaks or leave a visible reminder (e.g., leave your to-do list on your chair when you leave the office for lunch).

Past experiences: _____

Obstacles: _____

Use it More: _____

U   T   *Ask someone's opinion.* Show someone how you're doing and ask what he thinks. Maybe even ask him to push you a bit, to ask the harder questions that he might not otherwise have done. (A good therapist or coach will do this automatically.) If you hear something that you don't want to hear, remind yourself that it may save you more work in the long-run.

Past experiences: _____

Obstacles: _____

Use it More: _____

U   T   *Plan more regular check-ins at work.* You may find it helpful to break long projects into several smaller pieces and to check in with your boss and/or coworkers more often. The idea is to make sure that everyone is pointed in the right direction and to prevent too much time being wasted going down the wrong path. It's better to make a change sooner rather than later. These meetings could be very quick and well worth the time.

Past experiences: _____

Obstacles: _____

Use it More: _____

U   T   *Check-in regularly with your romantic partner.* Busy couples/families especially need these designated times to check-in with each other, because otherwise too much happens between conversations. This results in too many unilateral decisions being made where the other person would have wanted some input. The goal of the family meetings is to keep everyone on the same page and making well-informed, well thought-out decisions.

Past experiences: _____

Obstacles: _____

Use it More: _____

Key Concept: Reflect upon lessons learned.

U T *Plan in de-briefing time.* Build in some time to think about a completed project and what went well, what didn't go as well, what you would do differently next time, lessons learned, etc. Try to do this soon after the project (or along the way for longer projects) so the memories are still fresh.

Past experiences: _____

Obstacles: _____

Use it More: _____

U T *Talk it through with a professional.* In addition to helping you beforehand as well as along the way, a therapist or coach can be a great sounding board to help you think through what has already happened. This could be events from earlier in the day or twenty years ago (especially if you're repeating a similar pattern).

Past experiences: _____

Obstacles: _____

Use it More: _____

U T *Keep a journal.* The act of writing in a journal forces us to think about what has been happening during our days. They can be a great opportunity to discover some worthy lessons or ideas for future situations, especially if they can help you see beyond the immediate situation.

Past experiences: _____

Obstacles: _____

Use it More: _____

U T *Create a to-do list, schedule, and/or materials list for repeating activities.* This is especially helpful for activities that you don't do as often. For example, I have a packing list on my computer that includes all the chargers, cables, etc. that I need when I present. Each time, I cross out some items and scribble down some others to customize it. These sorts of written records make it so that we don't need to reinvent the wheel each time (or at least try to remember it). It also makes it less likely that you will forget a step or item or not leave enough time.

Past experiences: _____

Obstacles: _____

Use it More: _____

U T *Generally seek feedback.* New York City had a mayor named Ed Koch who was famous for regularly asking, "How am I doing?" It's a great attitude to have and will provide you with a lot of good information. People tend to go with vague generalities ("that was good") unless you push them for more specifics. Everybody will have their own opinion about things, but you should begin to hear some trends. If nothing else, someone else's opinion may spur some good thinking on your part.

Past experiences: _____

Obstacles: _____

Use it More: _____

Your Own Hindsight and Forethought Strategies

There's a lot to be learned from past experiences. If it worked once, it might work again. Perhaps you kind of drifted away from a habit that was actually pretty good. Maybe you got bored with it. Maybe your habit got interrupted and you never came back to it. It happens. So maybe you just need to blow the dust off and use it again.

Think back on your past experiences over the years. What strategies have you used that have been helpful in making the most of your hindsight and forethought? Even though no strategy works perfectly, there had to be some that you used that were helpful and increased your batting average. And if they were helpful, they were probably consistent with the strategies that make the most of people's hindsight and forethought. Understanding how that works makes it more likely that you can apply them effectively to future challenges.

So let's identify those good strategies, understand how they are based in how your hindsight and forethought functions, and then apply them forward. It might be helpful to think about how a particular strategy fits into the key concepts for hindsight and forethought strategies, so I've included them below, as well. We'll answer the same questions that we did above.

Under each key concept, write out:

1. What strategy did you use?

2. How did this strategy work for you in the past?

3. What obstacles might get in the way of you using this strategy more often now?

4. How or where could you use this strategy more often?

Key Concept: Intentionally pause before reacting and then consider your options.

Strategy: _____

Past Experiences: _____

Obstacles: _____

Use it More: _____

Strategy: _____

Past Experiences: _____

Obstacles: _____

Use it More: _____

Key Concept: Make a point of seeing how you're doing occasionally and then adjust as needed.

Strategy: _____

Past Experiences: _____

Obstacles: _____

Use it More: _____

Strategy: _____

Past Experiences: _____

Obstacles: _____

Use it More: _____

Key Concept: Reflect upon lessons learned.

Strategy: _____

Past Experiences: _____

Obstacles: _____

Use it More: _____

Strategy: _____

Past Experiences: _____

Obstacles: _____

Use it More: _____

Apply Your Strategies

Choose Your Targeted Strategies

Look back at the suggested strategies and your own strategies from above. Choose one to three strategies to work on first—pick a manageable number so you can do it well. You may want to look back at the section on Fallout from Hindsight and Forethought Weaknesses (page 142) and match your strategies to your struggles.

Although it's tempting to jump headfirst into the deep end and start with the places that you're struggling the most, it may be worth getting your feet wet on some smaller and more manageable struggles first. These easier successes will teach you some helpful lessons that you can use when tackling the thornier problems. There's also nothing like success as a motivator.

⭐ Write down which strategies you are planning to try first:

1. _____
2. _____
3. _____

It's better to focus on just a few changes first. Once you have these down, come back and add in some other strategies.

4. _____
5. _____
6. _____
7. _____
8. _____

Create Opportunities to Practice

Practice makes perfect. Or at least better. Although it's likely that your life will throw you plenty of opportunities to apply these new strategies, it can also be helpful to intentionally create or anticipate situations to practice these strategies.

Strategy: *Schedule times to do specific tasks*

When and where can I apply this strategy? *Schedule an hour on Monday mornings to check the status of my various work projects.*

How do I know that this strategy is working? *I'm more on top of my projects and find out sooner when something is falling behind or hitting snags*

Strategy: _____

When and where can I apply this strategy? _____

_____

How do I know that this strategy is working? _____

_____

Strategy: _____

When and where can I apply this strategy? _____

_____

How do I know that this strategy is working? _____

_____

Strategy: _____

When and where can I apply this strategy? _____

_____

How do I know that this strategy is working? _____

_____

Make the Commitment

Once you have your targeted strategies identified, you need to make a commitment to apply them. A strategy is only as good as your commitment. Because this is a workbook, you only have yourself to answer to (which is ultimately all you have even when someone else is involved). I can guarantee that the strategies in this book, and probably most of the strategies you come up with, are good ones. They will get the job done. It all comes down to using them.

So I encourage you to take the pledge below. But don't do this lightly—think about it. Maybe take a day or a week to think about it. If you're going to do this, give it your best effort. You deserve it.

My Pledge

I want a better life, so I commit to:

- ■ Taking chances and trying something new.

- ■ Doing my best to use these strategies diligently, even when I don't feel like it.

- ■ Being open to learning from these experiences.

- ■ Being flexible when a strategy isn't working.

- ■ Only abandoning a strategy when I can replace it with another strategy that may work better.

_____

Signature   Date

See the Rewards

We're more likely to start and maintain behaviors that are being rewarded, so let's talk about those all-important rewards. They come in a number of different shapes and sizes, so let's not miss any—the more rewards, the better.

Automatic Rewards

Some rewards are directly tied to our behavior. For example:

- ■ *Inherent feelings of satisfaction/pride.* Even if no one else notices, we notice and feel good about having done something well.

- ■ *Natural consequences.* These are rewards that come from the world around us, like when someone offers a compliment. Or getting a good seat at the movies by showing up early.

It may be helpful to make a point of looking for and noticing these rewards. The hectic pace of life makes it easy to miss them—which then makes it easier to drop off from those good habits, even when they're working. Since you're more likely to find what you're actively looking for, let's identify what these rewards would be.

If I used these strategies diligently, I would feel:

_____

_____

_____

_____

_____

_____

_____

_____

_____

_____

If I used these strategies diligently, I would expect these natural consequences:

_____

_____

_____

_____

_____

_____

_____

_____

_____

_____

Reward Yourself

Sometimes the inherent rewards and natural consequences aren't enough to push us over the edge to do something. This is when self-administered rewards come in handy. For example, "I will let myself do some actual woodworking after I clean up my shop." Or "I can check the sports scores after I finish these work emails."

Sometimes the reward is a good thing, whereas at other times the reward is just less bad than the first task. For example, "I will read this magazine article after I finish that technical report." Starting with the less desirable task creates an incentive to get to the more desirable task.

Think about some rewards that you can put in place for using your strategies. The reward needs to be good enough that it is actually motivating (but not so good that you'll skip the work and just take the reward).

If I use these strategies consistently, I will earn these rewards:

_____

_____

_____

_____

_____

_____

_____

_____

_____

_____

Fine-tune Your Approach

Learn from Setbacks

You may find that it's much harder than you thought to apply your targeted strategies and make progress on the struggles that you first decided to focus on. This is normal and often expectable. Life is a constant process of trying things and learning from the feedback. If you get stuck, take a few moments to think about it and learn some valuable lessons.

Why was this harder than I expected?

_____

_____

_____

_____

_____

_____

_____

_____

_____

What obstacles are getting in my way?

_____

_____

_____

_____

_____

_____

_____

_____

_____

_____

What lessons have I learned from this?

_____

_____

_____

_____

_____

_____

_____

_____

_____

_____

What would need to change in order to make it worth attempting this again?

_____

_____

_____

_____

_____

_____

_____

_____

_____

_____

Hindsight and Forethought: Using the Past and Future to Guide the Present

How can I apply these lessons to my next efforts?

_____

_____

_____

_____

_____

_____

_____

_____

_____

Based on these lessons, what would be a good area to focus on next?

_____

_____

_____

_____

_____

_____

_____

_____

_____

_____

The Big Picture: Refine Your Approach

As we talked about in Chapter 3: Reality-Based Motivation, we learn from our experiences and apply those lessons forward. Life is a constant learning process. Now that you've been applying your targeted strategies for a few days or weeks, what lessons have you learned? If you take a few moments, I guarantee you will come up with some productive ideas, even if you've already done this a few times in other chapters. As you keep moving through the workbook, you will continue to figure out new things.

SECTION II Make Your Life Better

Lessons learned about my strategies:

_____

_____

_____

_____

_____

_____

_____

_____

_____

Lessons learned about how my brain works:

_____

_____

_____

_____

_____

_____

_____

_____

_____

_____

Lessons learned about how I motivate myself:

_____

_____

_____

_____

Hindsight and Forethought: Using the Past and Future to Guide the Present

_____
_____
_____
_____
_____

Lessons learned about my workplace:

_____
_____
_____
_____
_____
_____
_____
_____
_____
_____

Lessons learned about my home life:

_____
_____
_____
_____
_____
_____
_____
_____
_____

SECTION II   Make Your Life Better

Lessons learned about using this workbook:

_____

_____

_____

_____

_____

_____

_____

_____

_____

_____

CHAPTER 12

STRIVE FOR PERSISTENCE, NOT PERFECTION

Living with ADHD is a process.

As with most of the big things in life, there are no quick and easy answers. Rather, progress involves continually making refinements in how we approach challenges. Sometimes we find a better way to do the same old things. Sometimes we need to start with the same old strategies to deal with a new situation. Life keeps moving, so we need to keep adapting and learning. This makes for more work, but it also makes it much more interesting. (Seriously, who wants eighty identical years?)

As you move through life and keep working on your ADHD, you may find that you're reminded of some of the strategies or exercises from this workbook. Or you realize that a strategy that didn't fit well into your life at the time now works better for you as your circumstances change. You may also find that as you continue to learn more about ADHD specifically and how you function generally, you understand the executive functions and these strategies at a deeper level. The nuances make more sense. You really get it.

This is all good. Go with it.

As a result, you may find that you return to the workbook from time to time. You may go back through the exercises that you've already done but apply the lessons differently because the demands in your life have changed. Or you may try some exercises, strategies or chapters that now seem more relevant to your life. It's interesting to see how our perspective changes over time as our understanding grows. As you continue to learn more about your ADHD, you may find that you get more out of the exercises than you did the first time.

This Is Important Stuff

A friend and fellow psychologist, Roberto Olivardia, recently sent me and Stephanie Sarkis an email that included a blog post from a woman who had seen him present on ADHD and eating disorders at the National CHADD conference. She wrote about what a profound moment it was for her to realize how her undiagnosed ADHD was driving her problems with eating. Suddenly, sitting in the audience, all the pieces fell into place for her and it set her on a much better path. This happens a lot when adults with ADHD are finally diagnosed.

Obviously, Roberto was really happy to see that his presentation had such a positive effect. We traded some emails about how great it is to see this sort of thing. It's really gratifying to see someone take an idea, whether it's from a therapy session, book, or presentation, and do something good with it. There's a real sense of pride in it, but we also carry a deep sense of responsibility. When people come to a therapy session, pick up a book, or attend a presentation, they are at a crossroads. Their lives may stay the same, and perhaps an opportunity is lost, or maybe something really clicks and they veer off down a whole new path in life that offers more opportunities than they could have predicted beforehand. So there's great potential, but the therapist and client, author and reader, presenter and audience all have to do their part.

This is important stuff we've been working on together in this workbook. There's a lot at stake—your happiness, your self-esteem, your performance at work/school, and even your romantic partner's happiness.

I worked really hard to give you information that is scientifically valid, yet useful in your daily life. I want you to do better and feel better. You don't get to choose whether you have ADHD, but you do get to choose what you do about it. I appreciate the hard work that you've put into applying the lessons from this workbook in order to make the changes that matter in your life. I know it wasn't easy; I will assume that it was worth it.

No matter how hard you worked, I know that everything won't be perfect today. That's OK. What really matters is that you feel a sense of optimism and enthusiasm as you work towards a better tomorrow.

If we can achieve that, this workbook has been a success, and you should feel proud.